Mastering Modes
for Guitar

by Ed Lozano and Joe Dineen

Amsco Publications
New York/London/Paris/Sydney/Copenhagen/Madrid/Tokyo/Berlin

Cover photography by Randall Wallace
Project editor: Ed Lozano
Interior design and layout: WR Music Service

Order No. AM 971454
US International Standard Book Number: 0.8256.1903.3
UK International Standard Book Number: 0.7119.8981.8

Exclusive Distributors:
Music Sales Corporation
257 Park Avenue South, New York, NY 10010 USA
Music Sales Limited
8/9 Frith Street, London W1D 3JB England
Music Sales Pty. Limited
120 Rothschild Street, Rosebery, Sydney, NSW 2018, Australia

Printed in the United States of America by
Vicks Lithograph and Printing Corporation

Table of Contents

CD Track List

1. Tuning Track

The Relative Approach
2. Major (Study Track)
3. Major (Practice Track)
4. Jazz Minor (Study Track)
5. Jazz Minor (Practice Track)
6. Harmonic Minor (Study Track)
7. Harmonic Minor (Practice Track)
8. Harmonic Major (Study Track)
9. Harmonic Major (Practice Track)
10. Tonal Pentatonic (Study Track)
11. Tonal Pentatonic (Practice Track)
12. Semitonal Pentatonic Type 1 (Study Track)
13. Semitonal Pentatonic Type 1 (Practice Track)
14. Semitonal Pentatonic Type 2 (Study Track)
15. Semitonal Pentatonic Type 2 (Practice Track)

The Parallel Approach
16. Major (Study Track)
17. Major (Practice Track)
18. Jazz Minor (Study Track)
19. Jazz Minor (Practice Track)
20. Harmonic Minor (Study Track)
21. Harmonic Minor (Practice Track)
22. Harmonic Major (Study Track)
23. Harmonic Major (Practice Track)
24. Tonal Pentatonic (Study Track)
25. Tonal Pentatonic (Practice Track)
26. Semitonal Pentatonic Type 1 (Study Track)
27. Semitonal Pentatonic Type 1 (Practice Track)
28. Semitonal Pentatonic Type 2 (Study Track)
29. Semitonal Pentatonic Type 2 (Practice Track)

Advanced Scales
30. Blues Scale Type 1 (Study Track)
31. Blues Scale Type 1 (Practice Track)
32. Blues Scale Type 2 (Study Track)
33. Blues Scale Type 2 (Practice Track)
34. Blues Scale Type 3 (Study Track)
35. Blues Scale Type 3 (Practice Track)
36. Whole Tone (Study Track)

37. Whole Tone (Practice Track)
38. Symmetrical Diminished Type 1 (Study Track)
39. Symmetrical Diminished Type 1 (Practice Track)
40. Symmetrical Diminished Type 2 (Study Track)
41. Symmetrical Diminished Type 2 (Practice Track)
42. Major Bebop (Study Track)
43. Major Bebop (Practice Track)
44. Minor Bebop (Study Track)
45. Minor Bebop (Practice Track)
46. Dominant Bebop (Study Track)
47. Dominant Bebop (Practice Track)

Ethnic Scales
48. Gypsy Minor (Study Track)
49. Gypsy Minor (Practice Track)
50. Neapolitan Minor (Study Track)
51. Neapolitan Minor (Practice Track)
52. Hirajoshi (Study Track)
53. Hirajoshi (Practice Track)
54. Kumoi (Study Track)
55. Kumoi (Practice Track)
56. In (Study Track)
57. In (Practice Track)
58. Tanzanian (Study Track)
59. Tanzanian (Practice Track)
60. Congolese (Study Track)
61. Congolese (Practice Track)
62. Bhairava (Study Track)
63. Bhairava (Practice Track)
64. Pooravi (Study Track)
65. Pooravi (Practice Track)
66. Marava (Study Track)
67. Marava (Practice Track)
68. Kanakangi (Study Track)
69. Kanakangi (Practice Track)
70. Pelog (Study Track)
71. Pelog (Practice Track)

Modal Usage
72. Major Modal Vamp
73. Minor Modal Vamp
74. Dominant Modal Vamp

Acknowledgements

Joe Dineen would like to thank:
- My wife, the inspiration of my life, Jennifer Crammer, for just about everything but most especially the meaning of the word love.
- Ed Lozano for bringing me along on this journey, his knowledge, and for the great friend that he has been for the last 25 years.
- Dan Earley and Peter Pickow for their high caliber of professionalism.
- Dan Axelrod for teaching me that the most essential elements in music are its honesty, enjoyability, and the ability to swing.

Ed Lozano would like to thank:
- Joe Dineen for his musicianship, creative suggestions, and support. But most importantly, for his friendship.
- My two mentors: Peter Pickow and Dan Earley.
- All of the folks at Music Sales Corporation.
- Susan and Jim Cavanaugh from Black Diamond Strings.
- My family and friends.
- The countless number of musicians whose recordings have been an education and inspiration.
- And finally, to the Creator for all of the above and then some. I humbly *gassho* before you.

Preface

Modes have always been an intriguing topic for debate among guitarists. Once you decide to become serious about guitar playing it seems that the next step is to understand modes. After all, you already have a working knowledge of scales, arpeggios, and chords. The problem is that those who do understand modes can't seem to explain how to use them.

So where do you go? The music store bins are filled with some very good books that illustrate fretboard maps and scale frames with different modes in different positions, using different fingerings, with different theoretical approaches, *etc.*—but all you really want to do is make music.

I was faced with this dilemma the year before I began studying at Berklee College of Music. I sought out the local hot stick (a guy who had just graduated from Berklee) and his advice was, "learn your modes." So, I began my exploration of the uncharted territory of modes and just where they were hiding on my guitar's fretboard.

My friend (and co-author), Joe Dineen, was also undergoing a similar journey at about the same time. Reading those obscure books that were at the bottom of the music store shelf. You know, those books that didn't seem as fun as the "Rock Riffs and Tricks" type books or those that have your favorite bands songs transcribed note-for-note.

Both of our journeys paralleled each other in the search for a more user-friendly and less complicated method on how to use modes. We had both grown tired of "box patterns" and clichés that sound uninspired and predictable. We wanted to introduce an understandable, hands-on approach that would free up a player melodically. And after many years of lessons, clinics, workshops, and the countless hours of practice, we decided that a more practical approach to mode playing was necessary.

You hold in your hands the result of over forty years of professional experience—a practical guide to modal usage.

Introduction

Welcome to *Mastering Modes for Guitar*!

This method serves as a practical guide for understanding modes. We will accomplish this by addressing a few questions that have baffled many guitarists (and musicians in general):
*   *What are modes?*
*   *How are they built?*
*   *Why do they function as they do?*
*   *Where can I use them?*

How are we going to answer these questions?

To begin with, we will build a foundation by discussing some theory basics so that you can understand how scales and chords are constructed and related (this will answer three questions: what they are, how they're built, and why they function as they do). This is important because comprehending the musical language will enable you to better express yourself. And, the majority of misconceptions—especially when it comes to modes—stems from players not having a clear theoretical understanding of the subject. Don't worry, the discussion on music theory is fairly straight ahead. Once you understand the theory behind one scale you will understand them all.

Secondly, practice suggestions and patterns are included because it is important to know *how* to use modes before you can learn *where* to use them. In addition, there is a brief discussion on the history of modes. This is included for you curious souls who like to know a little bit more than the next player.

And finally, we will introduce these modes and offer two approaches that will help explain their application(s). All of the music examples are demonstrated on the accompanying CD with a backup band. You will also have an opportunity to practice with the specially designed play-along tracks. This provides a perfect venue for practicing what you have learned and/or developing new ideas. There is also an overview (discussed in the *How to Use This Book* section) for each mode that provides all of the pertinent information for each scale.

As an added feature we have included special sections on advanced and ethnic scales. Never before have all of these scales been compiled in one volume. This is truly the only scale book that you will ever need.

Beginners should not be intimidated by the topics discussed in this book as they are not as ominous as they sound. Likewise, intermediate and advanced players will also find plenty of ideas that will take their playing to new levels. In short, *Mastering Modes for Guitar* is a must for every guitarist looking to further their understanding of modes and scales while improving their melodic playing.

Basic Tablature and Standard Notation

The music in this book has been written in both guitar *tablature* and standard notation. The tablature system has had a long history dating back to the lute music of the Renaissance. Today's TAB system uses six horizontal lines; each line represents a string of the guitar, with string 1 being the highest and string 6 the lowest. The numbers that appear on our TAB staff indicate the fret position, while a zero indicates that the string should be played open.

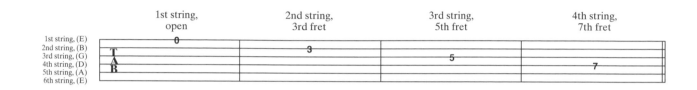

Tablature will only give you the pitch—you have to look at the standard notation to determine the duration of each note. Refer to the chart below for a breakdown of note values.

Chord and Scale Frames

The frames used to illustrate chords and scales are fairly easy to read. The frame depicts a portion of the guitar's fretboard. The vertical lines represent the strings of the guitar with the thickest string to the left and the thinnest to the right. The horizontal lines represent the frets. The nut of the guitar is represented by the bold horizontal line at the top of the diagram. If the top line is not bold then the frame represents a section of the middle of the fretboard with the exact location indicated by the fret number to the right of the frame. The dots that appear in the frames illustrate where you should place your fingers. An **X** above the top line indicates that that string should be muted or not played while an **O** above the top line indicates that that string should be played open.

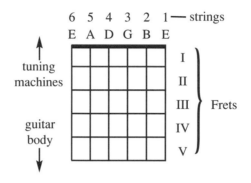

Music Theory Primer

Let's begin by discussing some basics. Music is a language and the better you understand the fundamental concepts of the language, the better you can communicate.

First, let's look at the musical alphabet. The staff below illustrates the notes available on the guitar.

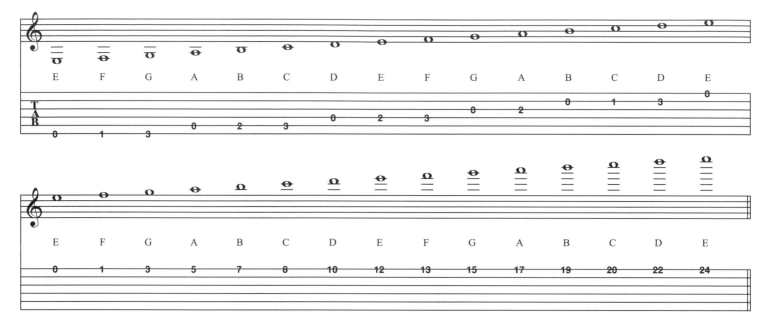

Notice that the letters that make up the note names repeat after every seven notes. The lowest note is an E which moves up to F and then up to G. At this point we go up again to the next note, which is A and the notes that ascend from this point on go up alphabetically from A to G. This cycle repeats itself until we run out of notes on the guitar.

Scales

The notes move up in a series of steps to form a *scale*. A *whole step* is the distance between two notes that are two frets apart, and a *half step* is the distance between any two adjacent notes. Take a look at the following example and notice that as the notes on the musical staff go up, so do the numbers on the tablature staff.

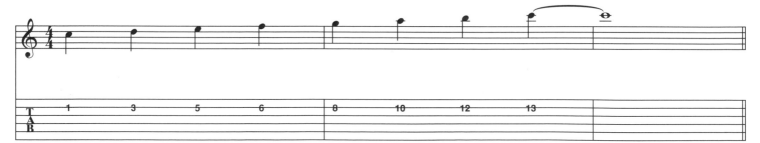

By changing the combination of whole steps and half steps we can change the scale type. We'll use the C major scale as our reference point. The chart below illustrates the scale with whole numbers and Roman numerals.

Diatonic

Diatonic means "belonging" to a scale; that is, if a group of notes all belong to a certain scale then they are diatonic to that scale.

Modes

A *mode* defines the selection of notes, arranged in a scale, that form the tonal substance of a piece of music. In any given key a large number of modes are possible. For example, playing all the white keys on a piano in ascending order from C to C gives you a C major sound; but more specifically, in the key of C major, the arrangement of notes from C to C gives you an Ionian mode (more on this in the next section). If you do the same exercise playing from D to D on the white keys of the piano you are still playing notes in the key of C major but the tonality of the notes played together sounds minor. The notes from D to D spell out a D Dorian mode.

To illustrate this point more clearly, try to imagine the sound of a C major scale as being a color—let's use blue. Then try to imagine all of the modes in C major as being different shades of blue. They still share the common color blue, but each mode is slightly darker or lighter than the next.

A simpler definition would be that a mode is basically a scale within a scale.

Chords

The Roman numerals refer to chords. A *chord* is made up of two or more notes played simultaneously. For example, a *C major triad* is made up of three notes; those three notes are scale degrees 1, 3, and 5—or notes C, E, and G.

Arpeggios

An *arpeggio* is simply a chord that has been broken into single notes.

Power Chords and Diads

Power chords and *diads* are two-note chords used in blues and rock. The most common ones are fifth, sixth, and seventh chords. For instance, a C5 diad is made up of scale degrees 1 and 5 (or notes C and G). A C6 diad is made up of scale degrees 1 and 6 (or notes C and A). A C7 diad is made up of scale degrees 1 and ♭7 (or notes C and B♭). These chord types are important for playing rock riffs and shuffle rhythms.

Progressions

A *progression* is a chord sequence or pattern. Just like two or more notes make up a chord, two or more chords make up a progression. In folk, rock, and blues music a progression is commonly made up of chords I, IV, and V. In the key of C these chords would be C, F, and G.

Key Signatures

The sharps and flats that are used in the construction of a particular scale or key are called the *key signature*. The key signature is placed at the beginning of a composition (at the left of the staff next to the clef) and eliminates the need to place the sharp or flat next to those notes in the composition.

Chord Charts and Leadsheets

Take a look at the diagram below.

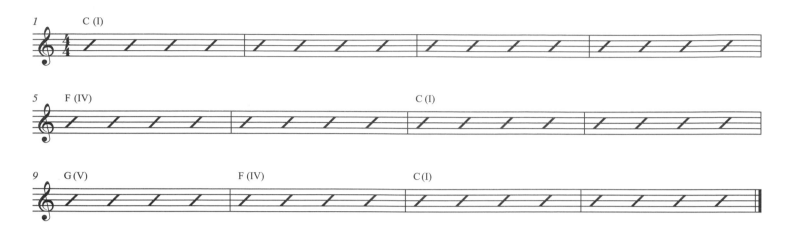

This is called a *chord chart*. It is very important to learn how to read these charts as they can guide you rather painlessly through an entire tune. Although this is just a basic twelve-bar blues progression, the chart helps you visualize what you should be playing.

The following chart contains some more complex notation but don't let that intimidate you.

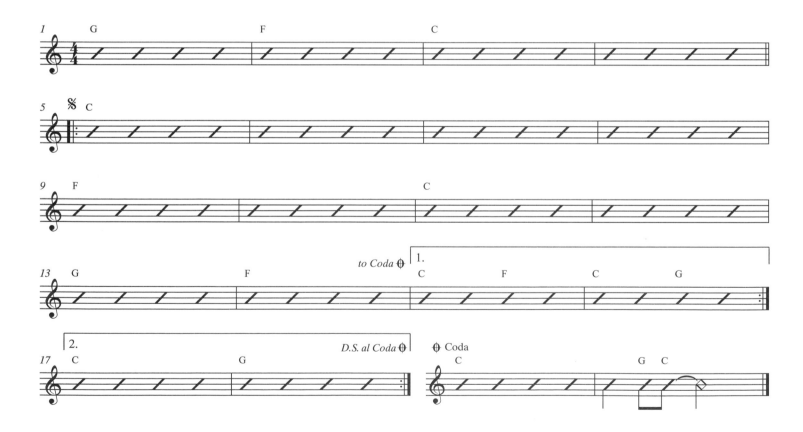

Now, let's go through the chart one step at a time:

- The *intro* consists of the first four *measures* or *bars*.
- The repeat sign (‖:) tells us that this is the measure that we repeat from when we reach this other repeat sign (:‖).
- Notice the twelve measures between repeat signs. This section is called the *verse* or *chorus*. In blues, these terms are interchangeable.
- The rhythm slashes that appear in each measure indicate that a rhythm pattern is being played but does not indicate a specific rhythm.
- The *first* and *second endings* indicate which ending to take depending on how many times you've played the section.
- The last two bars in a twelve-bar blues verse are often referred to as the turnaround. The *turnaround* is a descending (or ascending) pattern played at the end of a blues verse that brings you back to the top.
- The *segno* is the symbol (𝄋). *D.S. al Coda*⊕ *(Dal Segno al Coda)* indicates that you go back to the 𝄋, replay the section and then to the Coda (⊕).
- This symbol (‖) indicates the end of the tune.

A *leadsheet* is basically the same as a chord chart except that it includes the melody and the lyrics of the tune.

The Circle of Fifths

One of the basic principles governing the movement of chords is the fact that there is a strong tendency for a note to move down a perfect fifth (or up a perfect fourth). Notice below, in the C scale, the note G wants to move to the note C; whether down a perfect fifth or up a perfect fourth. Play G followed by the C on your instrument and you will hear this strong pull.

In the same way that G wants to go to C, C wants to go to F, F wants to go to B♭, and B♭ wants to go to E♭. This principle of notes wanting to move down a perfect fifth has come to be known as moving through the cycle (or circle) of fifths and is often illustrated as shown.

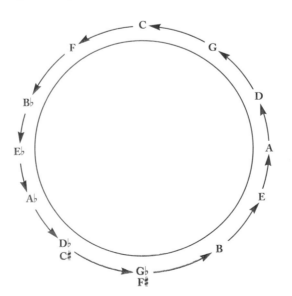

Each letter in the circle represents the root or letter name of a chord. The chords move in the direction shown by the arrows, so that a C chord moves to an F chord, an F chord moves to a B♭ chord, a B♭ chord moves to an E♭ chord, E♭ to A♭, and so on.

The chords represented by the letter names on the circle may all be of the same quality or of mixed qualities. However, great care must be taken so that chords remain within the framework of the diatonic scale. For example, if you want to use the circle to create a progression in the key of C, you must choose chords that have as their roots any of the letters on the circle that go from B to F. If you go beyond the F to the B♭ you are out of the key of C. Generally speaking, no more than four chords on the circle are used in any particular key. In the key of C that would be an A chord to a D chord to a G chord to a C chord.

Chromatic Cycle

The circle of fifths illustrates movement of a perfect fifth in one direction (clockwise) and a perfect fourth in the other direction (counterclockwise). In either case, by following the diagram you begin at the C note, chord, or key and end at the C note having played through all twelve notes, chords, or keys. The same principle can be used while playing through a chromatic cycle simply by moving in half steps (either ascending or descending) until you arrive at the next C note an octave above (or below).

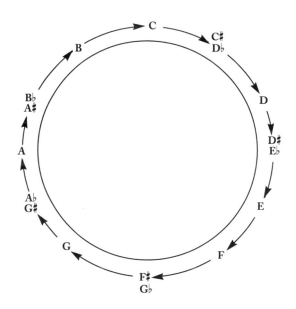

How to Use This Book

The purpose of this book/CD method is to help you develop a comprehensive understanding of modes, advanced and ethnic scales, and their usage. All of the examples are played with a backing band and there is a backup track for you to play along. The backup track has a rhythm guitar, keyboards, bass guitar, and drums. These tracks provide you with the opportunity to practice in a "live" atmosphere.

For those of you who are new to music we've included explanations of tablature, music notation, chord and scale frames, along with some basic theory. Although these sections help us to understand some musical terms and principles of theory, it is not intended as a formal text. For those of you interested in exploring music theory more in depth we would suggest *Theory & Harmony for the Contemporary Musician* by Arnie Berle (AM931360) published by Amsco.

You're probably itching to get started, but before you start playing we suggest listening to the CD while following along with your book. Learning to listen to the slight differences between modes will require some discipline. You can then practice with the example as it's playing or practice with the backup track provided. Each example has a count off so that you'll know when to start playing. Set the backup track to repeat and play for as long as you like. We encourage you to create your own licks, riffs, and ideas.

One of the primary features of this book is the "Scale Overview" that precedes each mode. This provides you with a quick reference guide that can be applied to any key. Let's take a closer look at the scale overview for the major scale below.

> Mode: Ionian
> Formula: 1 2 3 4 5 6 7 8
> Construction: W W H W W W H
> Chord Types: maj, 6, 6/9, maj7, maj9, maj13
> Diatonic Harmony: Imaj7, IIm7, IIIm7, IVmaj7, V7, VIm7, VIIm7♭5
> Key Signature: No sharps or flats (for the key of C)

The name of the mode is mentioned first followed by the formula. The *formula* illustrates the scale degrees that make up this mode. Next you'll find the *construction* which contains the arrangement of whole steps and half steps used to create this scale. (This will enable you to build this scale on any note.) This is followed by the *chord types* that this mode is most commonly used with; for example, melodies created by the Ionian mode will work well over the following chord types: maj, 6, 6/9, maj7, *etc*. Next you'll discover the *diatonic harmony* or all of the available chords that are constructed by this scale. Finally, we've included a *key signature formula* that provides you with a shortcut for figuring out the appropriate key signature (for a detailed explanation see the "Modal Key Signature" section).

Take a look at the next music example and notice that everything in the scale overview can be found in the music below.

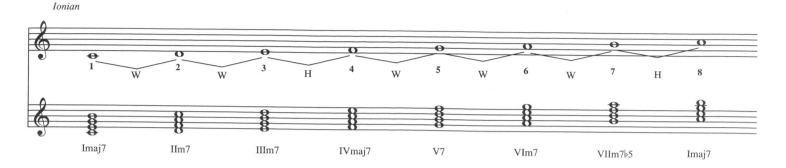

You'll notice that the first section is called "The Relative Approach." These are modes created by a common scale that is referred to as the scale of origin. By playing the same notes, but changing the starting note, the scale's formula changes and a different mode is created. For example, the C major scale is made up of seven different notes (or scale degrees). You can begin a scale on each of the seven scale degrees and create seven different modes. All of these modes are made up of the same notes as the C major scale and are, therefore, *related*. (This is explained in more detail in "The Relative Approach" section.)

Now, what would happen if you took the same seven modes that you created above but, rather than play them on each scale degree of the C major scale, use their formulas to build them on a C note. In other words, all seven modes created by the major scale would begin with a C note. You would then have modes that are parallel to each other. (This is discussed in further detail in "The Parallel Approach" section.)

The additional sections on advanced and ethnic scales are demonstrated using the parallel approach. These scales provide some interesting sounds but should be approached one at a time. The subtle variations that each scale provides can be overwhelming to some players' ears. This is simply because you're not used to hearing certain intervals and, at first, they may sound wrong. Don't worry, we've all gone through this and it will just take a little bit of time and practice before your ears and fingers become familiar with these "new" sounds.

The section at the end of this book, "Modal Usage," breaks down all of the scales into three different categories: major, minor, and dominant. Practice them over the simple grooves (on the CD) and you will begin to hear the subtle differences that each mode or scale creates. You'll then realize just how many different choices are available.

We devised this approach in an effort to fully understand modes and their applications for ourselves. When we found a common ground—that is illustrated in this book—we approached our colleagues, other players, and educators to share with them what we believed to be a comprehensive explanation of modes. The process inspired our playing and took us into new directions. We discovered that other musicians understood our explanations of modal applications and offered us some advice, constructive criticism, and, in some cases, new scales. I've also used this method with my students and have bypassed many obstacles when it comes to teaching this topic.

The problem with modes lies not in learning them but in learning where and how to use them. We have approached this topic from that standpoint. But before we go any further, there is something that needs to be addressed—*modal key signatures.*

Modal Key Signatures

If you think the topic of modes is the cause of much debate, then take a look at musicians' faces when you bring up the topic of *modal key signatures*.

Although many texts exist on music notation, there are not many that cover the actual topic of modal key signatures. Be that as it may, there do exist some basic rules to these key signatures.

All of the modes have a scale of origin and, therefore, a reference point. The seven standard modes that are created by the major scale have *that* major scale as a reference point. Since all of those scales are related to each other and share the same notes, they will also share the same key signature.

What about modes created by minor scales?

Although there are three minor scales that are used as scales of origin, there only exists one true minor scale—the natural minor. Therefore, all of the modes relative to any minor scale will share the natural minor key signature. Any alterations will be dealt with by using accidentals where needed.

Here are two basic rules:
• 	If the mode (or altered mode) has the *major* scale as its scale of origin, then use the *relative major key signature.*
• 	If the mode (or altered mode) has the *minor* scale as its scale of origin, then use the *relative natural minor key signature.*

Now a word about the formulas…

The formulas contained in the overview provide you with a quick reference for finding the key signature; however, it is not always as simple as just adding and subtracting sharps or flats. In some cases you will have to subtract a sharp and then add a flat; for example, the key of G major contains one sharp and to create a G Dorian mode you have to use the formula for Dorian. The formula states that to create a Dorian mode you need to add two flats. Since G major has a sharp then you need to subtract one sharp and then add a flat. Canceling the sharp equals adding a flat.

Let's take a look at one more example—D major (two sharps)—and we want to create a D Phrygian. Well, the formula for Phrygian states that you need to add four flats. First, we need to cancel the two sharps (this equals adding two flats). Second, we need to add two more flats. You now have the key signature for D Phrygian.

The tables below will show you how to find the relative scale of origin for the modes created by the major, jazz minor, harmonic minor, and harmonic major scales.

(M=major   m=minor   P=perfect)

Major Modes

	Down ▼	Up ▲	Key Signature	Alterations
Ionian	*Use parallel major*			
Dorian	M2	m7		
Phrygian	M3	m6		
Lydian	P4	P5		
Mixolydian	P5	P4		
Aeolian	M6	m3		
Locrian	M7	m2		

Jazz Minor Modes

	Down ▼	Up ▲	Key Signature	Alterations
JM Mode 1	M6	m3		♮6 & ♮7
JM Mode 2	M2	m7		♭2
JM Mode 3	P4	P5		♯5
JM Mode 4	P4	P5		♭7
JM Mode 5	P5	P4		♭6
JM Mode 6	M7	m2		♮2
JM Mode 7	M7	m2		♭4

Harmonic Minor Modes

	Down ▼	Up ▲	Key Signature	Alterations
HM Mode 1	M6	m3		♮7
HM Mode 2	M7	m2		♮6
HM Mode 3	*Use parallel major*			#5
HM Mode 4	M6	m3		#4 & ♮6
HM Mode 5	M3	m6		♮3
HM Mode 6	P4	P5		#2
HM Mode 7	M7	m2		♭4 & ♭♭7

Harmonic Major Modes

	Down ▼	Up ▲	Key Signature	Alterations
HMaj Mode 1	*Use parallel major*			♭6
HMaj Mode2	M2	m7		♭5
HMaj Mode 3	M3	m6		♭4
HMaj Mode 4	P4	P5		♭3
HMaj Mode 5	P5	P4		♭2
HMaj Mode 6	P4	P5		#2 & #5
HMaj Mode 7	M7	m2		♭♭7

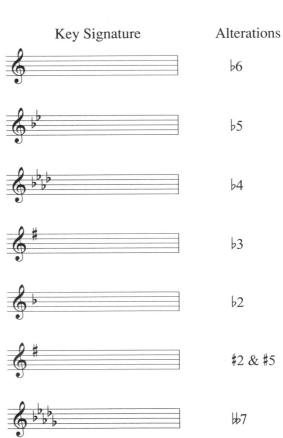

How to Practice

Scale practice is a perfect form of musical exercise. You work on finger dexterity and coordination between both hands while developing speed, strength, and endurance. Additionally, you train and develop your musical ear while gaining rhythmic discipline. These benefits occur more or less naturally when you practice regularly and correctly. There is no "one" correct way to practice; basically, you develop your own practice method. However, we will discuss some suggestions that will help you get organized. And once you are organized, you should stick to your routine.

I would like to add that I don't believe in pointless exercises, "guitar aerobics," or "chop-builders" as they do not necessarily have musical value—and our goal is to be *musical*. For whatever technique that you are trying to develop, there exists a real piece of music that will help you address that problem area. Remember that when you're improvising, people would prefer to hear a melodic line—and it can be flashy—rather than mindless exercises. You want to develop a routine that can be easily adapted to real-life playing situations.

So, here are some suggestions that will help you get started. Although some of these are general, be sure to pay careful attention to them as you will eventually be adding most, if not all, of these suggestions to your personal routine.

- Devote a percentage of your daily practice to scales; *e.g.*, if you practice for an hour a day, then devote fifteen or twenty minutes of that time to scale study.

- Begin with something that is easy and familiar—say, the C major scale and move it up and down the fretboard chromatically or through the circle of fifths.

- Sing the scale as you play it. The benefits of this could be a book by itself, but here are a few: learn new fingerings and/or scales faster, develop ear-hand coordination, hear the lines before playing them (a must for all improvisers), and the list goes on.

- Try varying your articulation and phrasing. Play the scales staccato and then legato. Incorporate hammerons, pulloffs, bends, slides, *etc.*

- Use a metronome or a drum machine. Not only will this help in gauging your progress but, and more importantly, will guide your development of rhythm and tempo.

- Try varying the rhythmic patterns: play straight-eighth notes and swing-eighth notes, eighth-note triplets, sixteenths, *etc.*

- Use different scale sequences (we've included some of these in the next section).

- Use the scales to develop new right-hand techniques. Try double-, triple-, and quadruple-picking each note; or, explore fingerstyle patterns. If you choose familiar scale patterns then the left-hand will be automatic and you can concentrate on your right hand.

- Try learning one mode at a time, as Bill Evans once said, "It's better to practice one thing for twenty-four hours than to practice twenty-four things in one hour."

- Memorize the formula, construction, and chord types for a particular mode and then try to incorporate it in a solo.

If it's not coming out then you have to know when to stop practicing and play the gig. But you have to try new things on your gig. Someone once told me to try a play just one new line or concept in the course of a gig.
Mike Stern

Practice Patterns

The patterns below are examples of melodic and rhythmic sequences that will help you get the scales "under your fingers." These have been written out in an abbreviated form, because after the first two or three measures you will be able to decipher the direction of the pattern.

The Five-Fret Approach

Most of the fingerings begin with either the third or fourth finger and span a five-fret region of the fretboard. We refer to this as the *five-fret approach* and this approach allows you to play the mode from each scale degree at any point on the fretboard. The five-fret approach also allows you to negotiate position shifts easily thereby liberating the player from the standard "box-type" fingerings.

The main purpose of the five-fret approach is to unlock the fretboard and bring out more of the characteristic flavor created by these modes. You may find some of these fingerings and stretches a little awkward and/or difficult at first, but after playing a few of these scales you will see how well they lay out on the fretboard. Give it a try and if you still don't feel comfortable with them try using standard (in-position) fingerings. After all, the main goal is to make music.

All of the patterns are written for the C major scale. This is for the sake of simplicity. Once you learn the pattern it is easy to apply it to all of the scales. Give them a try.

But before we begin playing, please refer to the "Tuning Track" on the CD and tune up. You may use an electronic tuner as all of the examples have been tuned to A=440.

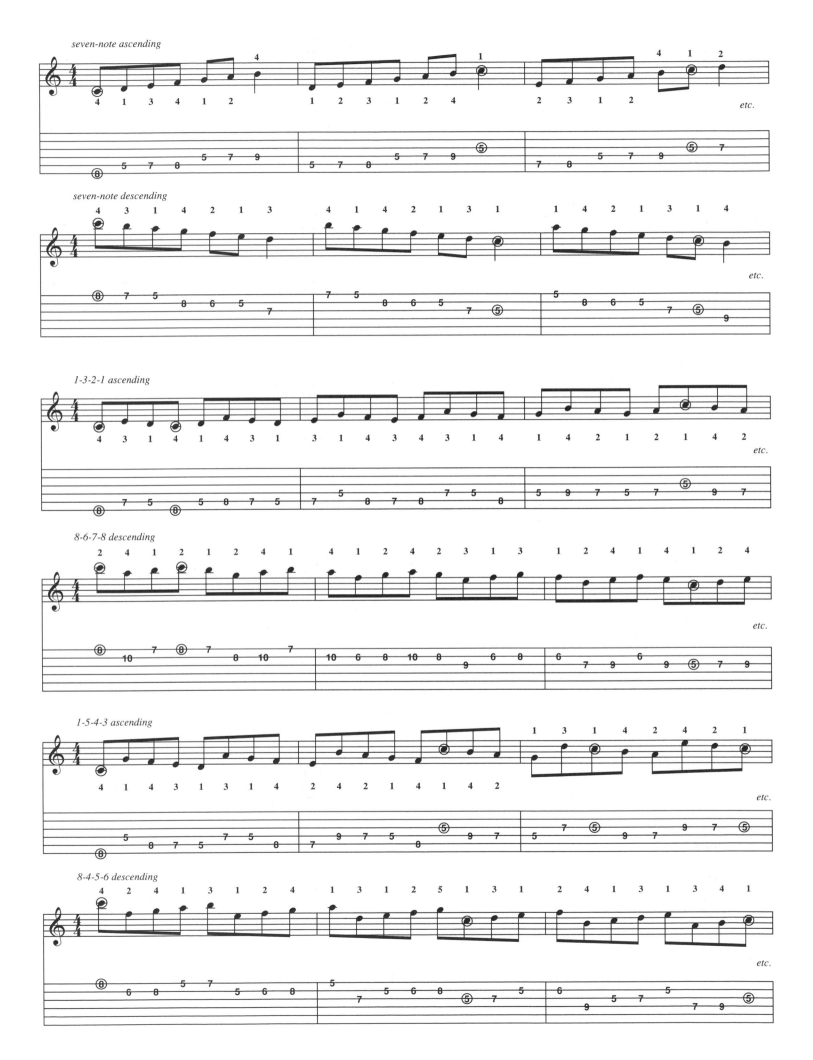

Modal History

Where do modes come from?

Good question. The answer, however, is subject to much debate.

Pope Gregory I (reigned 590–604) is believed to have developed the liturgical chant of the Roman Catholic Church. These chants have since been referred to as *Gregorian chants*. Now, the early development of the Gregorian chant has been researched back to Jerusalem and Antioch *c.* 385. Originally these chants were monotone in nature but eventually evolved into fully developed melodies. The tonality of the melodic chants subsequently came to be known as church modes. These church modes were given numbers which would appear at the beginning of the piece identifying its tonality or which mode is being used. The tonal basis for the Gregorian chant is this system of twelve church modes (see below).

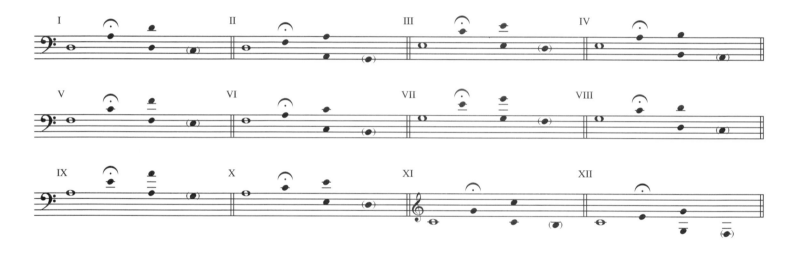

Where do the Greek names come from?

In ancient times the Greek theorists would debate the principles of music theory and had developed the "Greater Perfect System." This system was based on a fundamental tetrachord that was bounded by two notes a perfect fourth apart. (A *tetrachord* is the four scale degrees contained in a perfect fourth.) In between these two notes were two movable notes. The "Greater Perfect System" was based on the A Aeolian scale; however, they would alter the sixth tone by raising it a half step to conform to our modern day formula for the Dorian scale.

The argument would be that by changing the sequence of the notes—or more simply, by playing the same notes but from a different scale degree—the tonality would change. Subsequently, the modes from the major scale were formed and given names that refer to Greek cities.

It is important to note that the Greeks were not the only ones exploring modal theory, they were just the first to organize and agree on certain theoretical principles.

Introducing the Modes

There are only twelve notes; we can't invent new ones. It is all in the way we string the notes together and manipulate them in different ways.
Branford Marsalis

Below you'll find all of the modes built on a C note; or more specifically, with C as the tonic. Using the major scale as our basis you will clearly notice where all of the alterations occur in the scale. For each mode you will find a definition/description, a *formula* based on scale degrees (regulars whole numbers), *construction* which describes the arrangement of whole (W) and half (H) steps, the *chord types* or available harmony, *the diatonic harmony* or chords pertaining to that particular mode, as well as, the key signature formula. The chords are based on four-part harmony or seventh chords.

Scale of origin: Major

Although modes can be derived from any scale, the seven standard, or *authentic*, modes are built upon the major scale and, subsequently, they will serve as our starting point. Let's take a closer look at these modes.

Ionian is the modal name given for the major scale. The sound of this scale is the fundamental basis of most of our music. Ionian is built on the first degree of the major scale and is identified by the half steps that it contains between scale degrees 3 and 4, and scale degrees 7 and 8. This scale works well over any major chord.

Mode: Ionian
Formula: 1 2 3 4 5 6 7 8
Construction: W W H W W W H
Chord Types: maj, 6, 6/9, maj7, maj9, maj13
Diatonic Harmony: Imaj7, IIm7, IIIm7, IVmaj7, V7, VIm7, VIIm7b5
Key Signature: No sharps or flats (for the key of C)

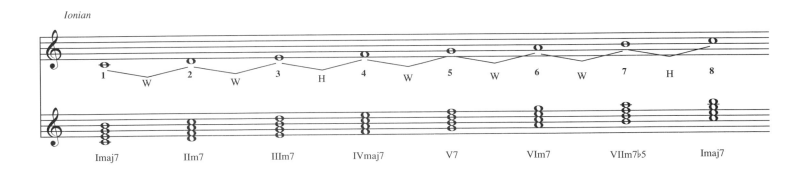

Dorian is a minor scale built on the second degree of the major scale. The sound produced by the note sequence of this scale is not quite as dark sounding as the natural minor (or *Aeolian*, see below) scale. This is due to the unaltered 6 degree in the Dorian scale. The natural minor scale has a ♭6 scale degree producing a "heavier" or darker sound. The Dorian mode has proved to be a favorite among today's rock and jazz players. The half steps in the Dorian mode occur between scale degrees 2 and 3, and scale degrees 6 and 7. This scale works well over most minor chords.

Mode: Dorian
Formula: 1 2 ♭3 4 5 6 ♭7 8
Construction: W H W W W H W
Chord Types: m, m6, m6/9. m7, m9, m13
Diatonic Harmony: Im7, IIm7, ♭IIImaj7, IV7, Vm7, VIm7♭5, ♭VIImaj7
Key Signature: Add two flats, or subtract two sharps

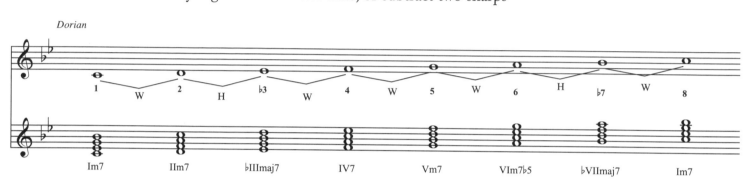

Phrygian is a minor scale built on the third degree of the major scale. Although the overall sound of this scale is minor, the ♭2 and ♭6 scale degrees produce an exotic flavor. In early music, this mode was used to create a solemn quality—and it is sometimes used for the same purpose in rock and heavy metal music today. However, the Phrygian mode is also used to add a distinctive Latin sound to pop and rock music. The half steps in the Phrygian mode occur between scale degrees 1 and 2, and scale degrees 5 and 6.

Mode: Phrygian
Formula: 1 ♭2 ♭3 4 5 ♭6 ♭7 8
Construction: H W W W H W W
Chord Types: m, m add♭9, m7, m7♭9, m(♭9,♭13)
Diatonic Harmony: Im7, ♭IImaj7, ♭III7, IVm7, Vm7♭5, ♭VImaj7, ♭VIIm7
Key Signature: Add four flats, or subtract four sharps

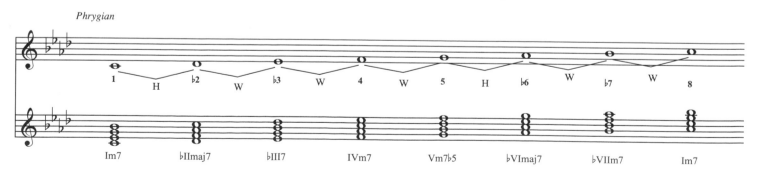

Lydian is a major sounding mode built on the fourth degree of the major scale. The sound created by this mode closely resembles the major scale with the exception of the ♯4 scale degree. The ♯4 (or *tritone*) creates a series of three whole steps from the root which invokes a sense of mystery. This mode is used by many jazz players over maj7 chords; however, rock and progressive-blues players also use this scale over the ♭VI chord in a minor progression. The half steps in the Lydian mode occur between scale degrees 4 and 5, and scale degrees 7 and 8.

Mode: Lydian
Formula: 1 2 3 ♯4 5 6 7 8
Construction: W W W H W W H
Chord Types: maj, maj add♯11, maj7♯11, maj13♯11
Diatonic Harmony: Imaj7, II7, IIIm7, ♯IVm7♭5, Vmaj7, VIm7, VIIm7
Key Signature: Add one sharp, or subtract one flat

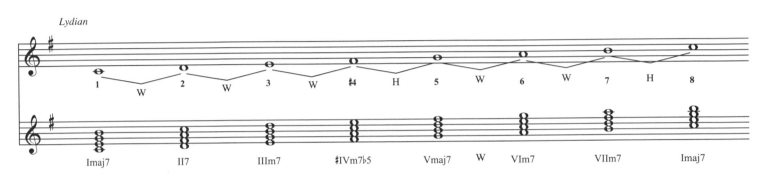

Mixolydian is a dominant sounding mode built on the fifth degree of the major scale. Although this mode is major in nature, the ♭7 scale degree distinguishes it from its major sounding sister modes. This mode has inspired many rock, blues, and jazz riffs and melodies; in addition, it is useful for improvising over dominant chords. The half steps in the Mixolydian mode occur between scale degrees 3 and 4, and scale degrees 6 and 7.

Mode: Mixolydian
Formula: 1 2 3 4 5 6 ♭7 8
Construction: W W H W W H W
Chord Types: sus4, 7, 9, 13, and all dominant sus4 chords
Diatonic Harmony: I7, IIm7, IIIm7♭5, IVmaj7, Vm7, VIm7, ♭VIImaj7
Key Signature: Add one flat, or subtract one sharp

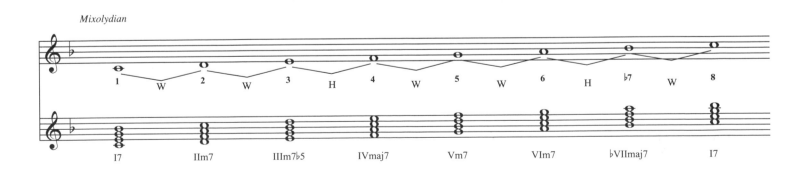

Aeolian is also known as the *natural minor scale* and is built on the sixth scale degree of the major scale. Although there are many other minor modes, the Aeolian mode is the most widely used of the minor sounding scales and considered to be the true minor tonality. That having been said, the Aeolian scale serves as the basis for minor scale harmony. The half steps in this mode occur between scale degrees 2 and 3, and scale degrees 5 and 6.

Mode: Aeolian
Formula: 1 2 ♭3 4 5 ♭6 ♭7 8
Construction: W H W W H W W
Chord Types: m, m add♭6, m7, m9, m11, m9♭13
Diatonic Harmony: Im7, IIm7♭5, ♭IIImaj7, IVm7, Vm7, ♭VImaj7, ♭VII7
Key Signature: Add three flats, or subtract three sharps

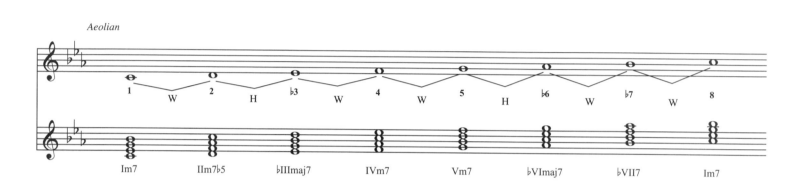

Locrian is built on the seventh degree of the major scale. This scale is constructed around a diminished triad or, more precisely, half-diminished seventh (m7♭5) chord therefore making its usefulness somewhat limited. However, the tension created by this mode make the Locrian scale a powerful tool for minor-key improvisation (as many jazz and jazz-fusion players have discovered). Progressive-blues artists have also successfully added this mode to substitution situations, and heavy metal players have also enjoyed the sinister sounds hidden in this scale. The half steps in this mode occur between scale degrees 1 and 2, and scale degrees 4 and 5.

Mode: Locrian
Formula: 1 ♭2 ♭3 4 ♭5 ♭6 ♭7 8
Construction: H W W H W W W
Chord Types: °, m7♭5
Diatonic Harmony: Im7♭5, ♭IImaj7, ♭IIIm7, IVm7, ♭Vmaj7, ♭VI7, ♭VIIm7
Key Signature: Add five flats, or subtract five sharps

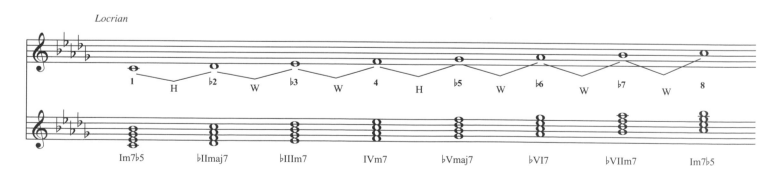

Scale of origin: Jazz Minor

Using the same principles, let's look at the modes that are based on the jazz minor scale.

The *jazz minor scale* is derived from the *melodic minor scale* found in traditional harmony. The melodic minor ascends in the same manner as does the jazz minor but descends using the natural minor scale degrees. Notice that the jazz minor shares the same formula as the major scale with the exception of the third degree. The third degree is lowered to give this mode an overall minor tonality. This difference of one note effects the tonality of the modes as well. Many jazz players from the post-Bop era use these modes as a departure point for their improvisations. These modes are a vital component of the modern jazz player's improvisational vocabulary and are sometimes referred to by the chord type that they are used with rather than the actual mode name. For example, JM Mode 3 would be called the maj7+ mode. (However, as we will discover, there exists more than one maj7+mode).

Modern players have tapped into the colorful sounds created by the modes from the jazz minor scale. Notice, however, that from this point on the chord types become somewhat limited. As we get further away from the major scale the harmonic applications of the modes become more and more specialized. Those daring enough to add these modes to their vocabulary will reap the benefits by sounding more hip, fresh, and creative.

Please note that the key signature formulas provide the modal tonality. These modes are *altered* and, as such, include *accidentals* so that they may conform to their "new" modality. For example, the key signature for a C JM Mode 1 includes three flats; however, the scale formula illustrates only one flat. Therefore, in order to create the JM Mode 1 sound, you will have to raise the 6 and 7 scale degrees by adding natural signs to them.

JM Mode 1 is the reference scale for the following other six modes. Composers and improvisers use this mode to construct melodies and solos used in a wide range of minor contexts. This mode is immediately recognized by the presence of the minor third and leading tone (scale degree 7).

> Mode: JM Mode 1
> Formula: 1 2 ♭3 4 5 6 7 8
> Construction: W H W W W W H
> Chord Types: m(maj7)
> Diatonic Harmony: Im(maj7), IIm7, ♭IIImaj7+, IV7, V7, VIm7♭5, VIIm7♭5
> Key Signature: Add three flats, or subtract three sharps

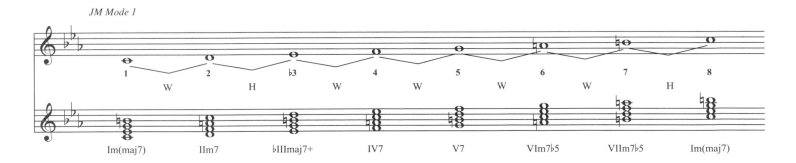

JM Mode 1

JM Mode 2 is also known as the *Dorian ♭2* or, less frequently, *Phrygian ♮6* (sometimes referred to as altered modes), depending on its intended harmonic application. This mode is primarily used as a compositional tool for adding an exotic flavor to the Dorian mode or a "lighter" color to the Phrygian mode. The debates begin with "JM Mode 2 is a Dorian sounding Phrygian scale" to "it's a Phrygian sounding Dorian scale." Let your ears be the judge. For our purposes, we will use the Dorian ♭2.

> Mode: JM Mode 2 (Dorian ♭2 or Phrygian ♮6)
> Formula: 1 ♭2 ♭3 4 5 6 ♭7 8
> Construction: H W W W W H W
> Chord Types: m7, m7♭9
> Diatonic Harmony: Im7, ♭IImaj7+, ♭III7, IV7, Vm7♭5, VIm7♭5, ♭VIIm(maj7)
> Key Signature: Add two flats, or subtract two sharps

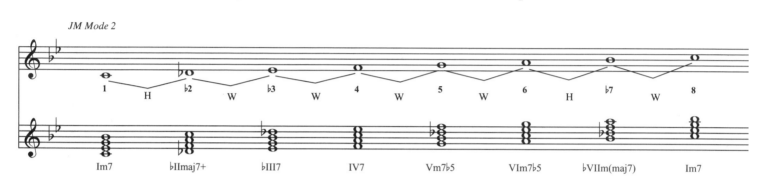

JM Mode 3 is known by its more famous modal name *Lydian ♯5*, or *Lydian augmented*. This mode shares the dominant properties of the whole tone scale with the major properties of the Ionian scale (primarily the sound of the major third and leading tone). Jazz players have popularized this mode and refer to it as the maj7+ mode. Cmaj7+ includes the same notes as an E/C (E triad with a C in the bass). In either case, this mode will work well as an improvisational or compositional tool.

> Mode: JM Mode 3 (Lydian ♯5)
> Formula: 1 2 3 ♯4 ♯5 6 7 8
> Construction: W W W W H W H
> Chord Types: maj7+
> Diatonic Harmony: Imaj7+, II7, III7, ♯IVm7♭5, ♯Vm7♭5, VIm(maj7), VIIm7
> Key Signature: Add one sharp, or subtract one flat

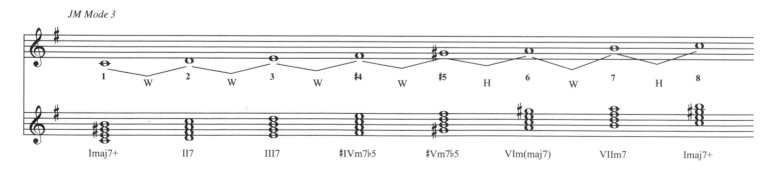

JM Mode 4 is known as *Lydian ♭7 (or Lydian dominant)*—the most popular of the altered modes. It is also sometimes (although less often) referred to as the Lydian mode (built on the fourth degree) of the jazz minor scale. By lowering scale degree 7 of the Lydian scale, the tonality of this mode is changed from major to dominant. This mode is a useful alternative to the Mixolydian mode. The Lydian ♭7 mode is primarily used by jazz players when improvising over dominant chords.

Mode: JM Mode 4 (Lydian ♭7)
Formula: 1 2 3 ♯4 5 6 ♭7 8
Construction: W W W H W H W
Chord Types: 7, 7♯11
Diatonic Harmony: I7, II7, IIIm7♭5, ♯IVm7♭5, Vm(maj7), VIm7, ♭VIImaj7+
Key Signature: Add one sharp, or subtract one flat

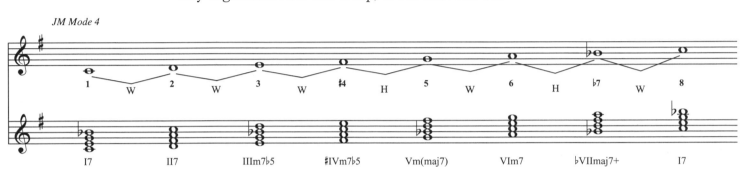

JM Mode 5 is sometimes called the *Mixolydian ♭6* mode. Another alternative to improvising over dominant chords, this mode is the darkest or heaviest sounding of the dominant modes. If Mixolydian has a neutral dominant sound, then Lydian ♭7 (JM Mode 4) has a brighter dominant sound and Mixolydian ♭6 (JM Mode 5) has a darker dominant sound.

Mode: JM Mode 5 (Mixolydian ♭6)
Formula: 1 2 3 4 5 ♭6 ♭7 8
Construction: W W H W H W W
Chord Types: 7, 7♭13
Diatonic Harmony: I7, IIm7♭5, IIIm7♭5, IVm(maj7), Vm7, ♭VImaj7+, ♭VII7
Key Signature: Add one flat, or subtract one sharp

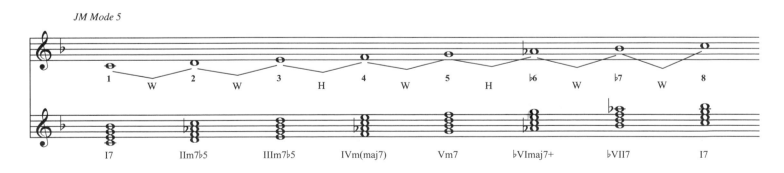

JM Mode 6, also known as *Locrian ♮2*, is constructed around a diminished triad and/or half-diminished seventh (m7♭5) chord. This mode has a somewhat more stable sound than the "unaltered" Locrian mode; subsequently, Locrian ♮2 (JM Mode 6) provides a less dissonant alternative to improvising and creating melodies over diminished and half-diminished chords.

Mode: JM Mode 6 (Locrian ♮2)
Formula: 1 2 ♭3 4 ♭5 ♭6 ♭7 8
Construction: W H W H W W W
Chord Types: °, m7♭5
Diatonic Harmony: Im7♭5, IIm7♭5, ♭IIIm(maj7), IVm7, ♭Vmaj7+, ♭VI7, ♭VII7
Key Signature: Add five flats, or subtract five sharps

JM Mode 6

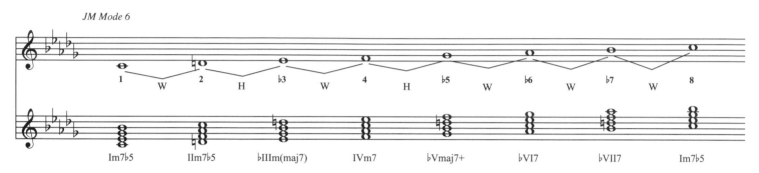

JM Mode 7 is also known as the *Super Locrian*; however, it is more appropriately called the *altered scale*. It is known as such because it contains the following colorful scale degrees: ♭9, ♯9, ♯11(or ♭5), and ♭13 (or ♯5). These altered scale degrees create an interesting sound to minor key dominant chords. The altered scale is a must for jazz and fusion players, although progressive blues and rock guitarists alike would benefit by adding this mode to their arsenal.

Mode: JM Mode 7 (Super Locrian or Altered Scale)
Formula: 1 ♭2(♭9) ♭3(♯9) ♮3 ♭5(♯11) ♭6(♭13) ♭7 8
Construction: H W H W W W W
Chord Types: m7♭5, 7, 7♭9, 7♯9, 7♯11, 7♭13, altered dominant chords in general
Diatonic Harmony: Im7♭5, ♭IIm(maj7), ♭IIIm7, IIImaj7+, ♭V7, ♭VI7, ♭VIIm7♭5
Key Signature: Add five flats, or subtract five sharps

JM Mode 7

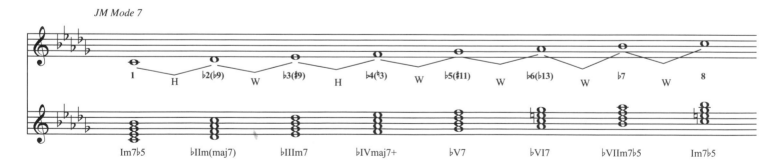

Scale of origin: Harmonic Minor

The *harmonic minor scale* is simply the natural minor scale with a raised seventh degree. This scale is immediately recognized by the minor third interval created by the raised seventh degree. The result is an exotic sounding minor scale that is popular in Eastern European folk, classically influenced rock, and jazz music alike.

The modes created from the harmonic minor scale are not as popular as those derived from the jazz minor but that does not diminish the importance of exploring the sounds hidden in this scale. Some players have found an exotic mode and made it part of their signature sound.

HM Mode 1, the first mode of the harmonic minor scale, is the primary choice of jazz players for soloing over m(maj7) chords. In addition, classically influenced guitarists such as Randy Rhoads and Yngwie Malmsteen launched the neo-classical fusion generation of guitarists in the 80s with the sounds created by this scale.

   Mode: HM Mode 1
   Formula: 1 2 ♭3 4 5 ♭6 7 8
   Construction: W H W W H m3 H
   Chord Types: m(maj7)
   Diatonic Harmony: Im(maj7), IIm7♭5, ♭IIImaj7+, IVm7, V7, ♭VImaj7, VII°7
   Key Signature: Add three flats, or subtract three sharps

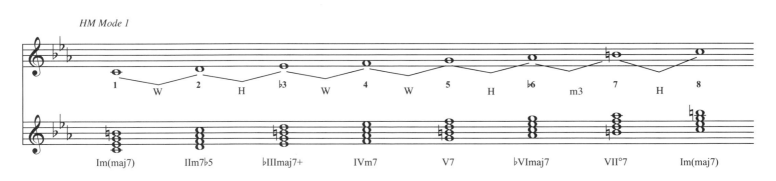

HM Mode 2 provides another alternative for creating melodies over diminished and m7♭5 chords. Notice the minor third interval between scale degrees ♭5 and 6.

Mode: HM Mode 2
Formula: 1 ♭2 ♭3 4 ♭5 6 ♭7 8
Construction: H W W H m3 H W
Chord Types: m7♭5
Diatonic Harmony: Im7♭5, ♭IImaj7+, ♭IIIm7, IV7, ♭Vmaj7, VI°7, ♭VIIm(maj7)
Key Signature: Add five flats, or subtract five sharps

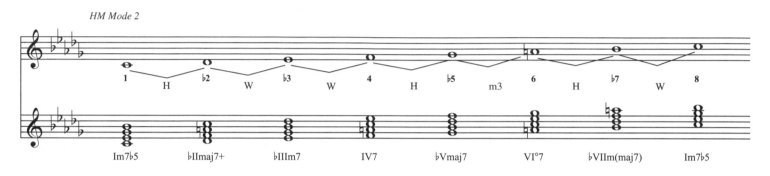

HM Mode 3 is also known as the maj7+ mode. It is more popular than its counterpart JM Mode 3 because of the interesting color found in the minor third interval and its less dissonant quality. This scale is popular among modern jazz players.

Mode: HM Mode 3
Formula: 1 2 3 4 ♯5 6 7 8
Construction: W W H m3 H W H
Chord Types: maj7+
Diatonic Harmony: Imaj7+, IIm7, III7, IVmaj7, ♯V°7, VIm(maj7), VIIm7♭5
Key Signature: No sharps or flats (for the key of C)

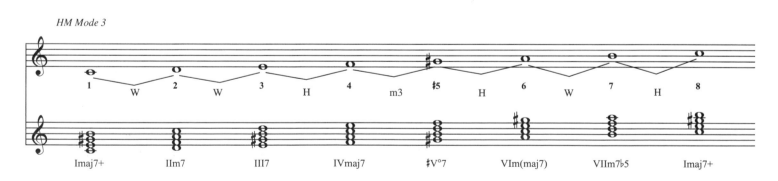

HM Mode 4 is built on the fourth degree of the harmonic minor scale. Depending on your note selection and phrasing, this mode can produce an exotic sound or a have a bluesy effect over a m7 chord.

Mode: HM Mode 4
Formula: 1 2 ♭3 ♯4 5 6 ♭7 8
Construction: W H m3 H W H W
Chord Types: m7
Diatonic Harmony: Im7, II7, ♭IIImaj7, ♯IV°7, Vm(maj7), VIm7♭5, ♭VIImaj7+
Key Signature: Add three flats, or subtract three sharps

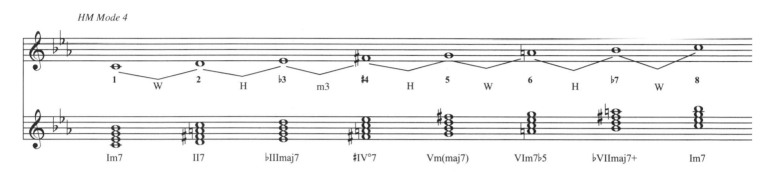

HM Mode 5 is known as the *Phrygian dominant* mode. This scale is used for creating melodies over a V7 chord in a minor key. Although the Phrygian dominant scale was popularized by the neo-classical fusion players of the modern era, this mode has been used for centuries in folk music all over the world. It can also be viewed as a Phrygian scale with a major third.

Mode: HM Mode 5 (Phrygian dominant)
Formula: 1 ♭2 3 4 5 ♭6 ♭7 8
Construction: H m3 H W H W W
Chord Types: 7, 7♭9, 7♭13
Diatonic Harmony: I7, ♭IImaj7, III°7, IVm(maj7), Vm7♭5, ♭VImaj7+, ♭VIIm7
Key Signature: Add four flats, or subtract four sharps

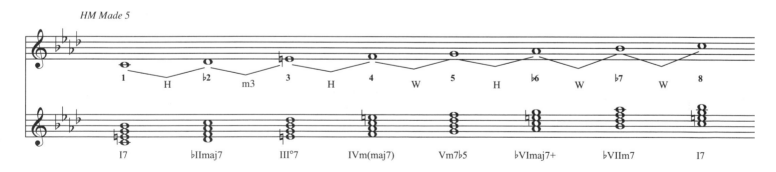

HM Mode 6 has a Lydian quality when you consider that it contains a ♯4 and major 7. The first interval, however, is a ♯2 and along with the ♯4 degree (as in HM Mode 4) can produce exotic and bluesy sounds. The ♯2 and ♯4 can function as a ♭3 and ♭5 thus producing a blues quality to a maj7 chord.

     Mode: HM Mode 6
     Formula: 1 ♯2 3 ♯4 5 6 7 8
     Construction: m3 H W H W W H
     Chord Types: maj7, maj7♯11
     Diatonic Harmony: Imaj7, ♯II°7, IIIm(maj7), ♯IVm7♭5, Vmaj7+, VIm7, VII7
     Key Signature: Add one sharp, or subtract one flat

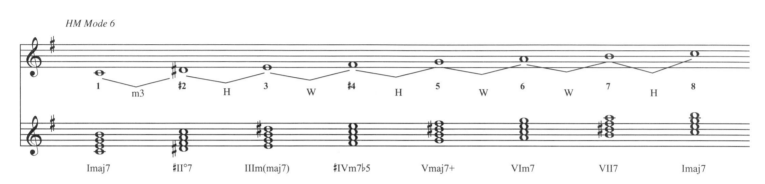

HM Mode 7 is interesting in that it contains a major third yet is played over a °7 chord. The quality of this scale is decidedly diminished and if the major third is treated as a passing tone it does not affect the tonality. This mode is rather limited in usefulness but can create some interesting sounds. Composers may find this scale more intriguing than improvisers.

     Mode: HM Mode 7
     Formula: 1 ♭2(♭9) ♭3(♯9) ♮3 ♭5(♯11) ♭6(♭13) ♭♭7 8
     Construction: H W H W W H m3
     Chord Types: °7
     Diatonic Harmony: I°7, ♭IIm(maj7), ♭IIIm7♭5, IIImaj7+, ♭Vm7, ♭VI7, ♭♭VIImaj7
     Key Signature: Add five flats, or subtract five sharps

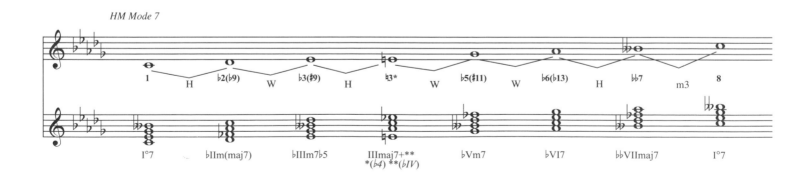

Scale of origin: Harmonic Major

The *harmonic major scale* is simply the major scale with a lowered sixth degree. This scale is immediately recognized by the minor third interval created by the lowered sixth and raised seventh degrees. The result is an exotic sounding major scale that has become popular in contemporary jazz music.

I first became aware of this scale from the contemporary jazz musicians playing in New York City's "downtown scene." The modes created from the harmonic major scale are not as popular as those derived from the previous scales but that is largely due to the fact that many players are simply unaware of this scale's existence. Let's explore these modes in further detail.

HMaj Mode 1, the first mode of the harmonic major scale, features a ♭6 and can also be viewed as an *Ionian ♭6 scale*. This mode serves as another alternative for creating melodies over a major chord. The minor third interval between the ♭6 and 7 give this scale its "harmonic" sound.

Mode: HMaj Mode 1 (Ionian ♭6)
Formula: 1 2 3 4 5 ♭6 7 8
Construction: W W H W H m3 H
Chord Types: maj7 add♭13
Diatonic Harmony: Imaj7 add♭13, IIm7♭5, III7♯9, IVm(maj7)add♯11, V7♭9, ♭VImaj7+, VII°7
Key Signature: No sharps or flats (for the key of C)

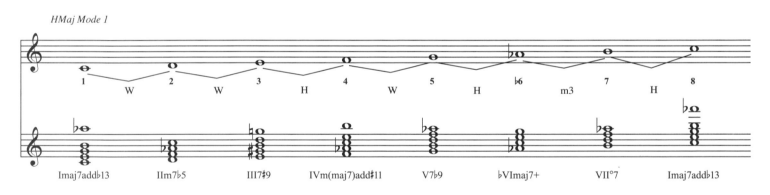

HMaj Mode 1

HMaj Mode 2 may also be viewed as a Dorian scale with a ♭5 and provides another alternative for creating melodies over m7, diminished, and m7♭5 chords. Notice the minor third interval between scale degrees ♭5 and 6. In addition, the ♭3, ♭5, and ♭7 create a bluesy sound over dominant chords.

Mode: HMaj Mode 2 (Dorian ♭5)
Formula: 1 2 ♭3 4 ♭5 6 ♭7 8
Construction: W H W H m3 H W
Chord Types: m7♭5
Diatonic Harmony: Im7♭5, II7♯9, ♭IIIm(maj7)add♯11, IV7♭9, ♭Vmaj7+, VI°7, ♭VIImaj7 add♭13
Key Signature: Add two flats, or subtract two sharps

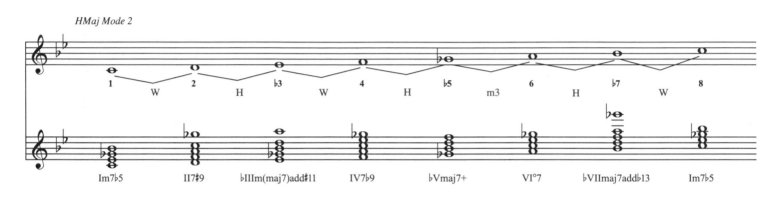

HMaj Mode 3 may also be viewed as a Phrygian scale with a ♭4. It has the characteristics of the Phrygian scale as it contains the ♭2, ♭3, ♭6, and ♭7 scale degrees. But the inclusion of the ♭4 (which functions as a ♮3) gives this scale a dominant sound or, to be more precise, an altered dominant sound.

Mode: HMaj Mode 3
Formula: 1 ♭2 ♭3 ♭4 5 ♭6 ♭7 8
Construction: H W H m3 H W W
Chord Types: 7♯9
Diatonic Harmony: I7♯9, ♭IIm(maj7)add♯11, ♭III7♭9, ♭IVmaj7+, V°7, ♭VImaj7 add♭13, ♭VIIm7♭5
Key Signature: Add four flats, or subtract four sharps

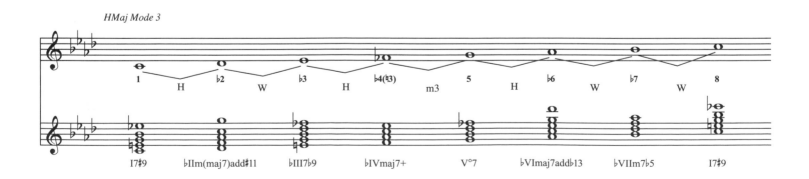

HMaj Mode 4 is built on the fourth degree of the harmonic major scale. This scale can also be viewed as a *Lydian minor scale* and creates an exotic sounding minor scale similar to the Gypsy minor (see "Ethnic Scales"). Therefore, it can also be viewed as a Gypsy minor with a ♮6. You can never have too many options for exotic sounding minor scales.

Mode: HMaj Mode 4 (Lydian minor)
Formula: 1 2 ♭3 ♯4 5 6 7 8
Construction: W H m3 H W W H
Chord Types: m(maj7)add♯11
Diatonic Harmony: Im(maj7)add♯11, II7♭9, ♭IIImaj7+, ♯IV°7, Vmaj7 add♭13, VIm7♭5, VII7♯9
Key Signature: Add one sharp, or subtract one flat

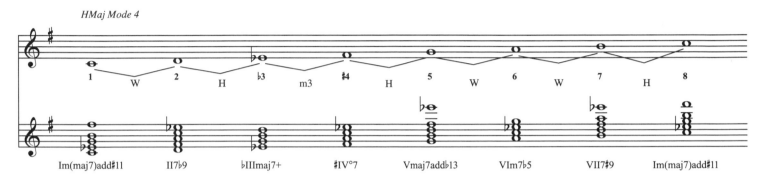

HMaj Mode 5 is another option for a dominant sounding mode. This scale is effective for creating melodies over a V7 chord in a minor key. It is sometimes referred to as the *7♭9 mode*.

Mode: HMaj Mode 5
Formula: 1 ♭2 3 4 5 6 ♭7 8
Construction: H m3 H W W H W
Chord Types: 7♭9
Diatonic Harmony: I7♭9, ♭IImaj7+, III°7, IVmaj7 add♭13, Vm7♭5, VI7♯9, ♭VIIm(maj7)add♯11
Key Signature: Add one flat, or subtract one sharp

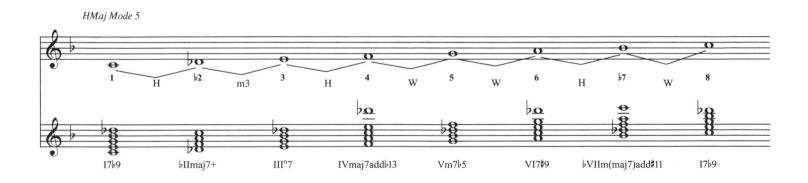

HMaj Mode 6 has a Lydian quality when you consider that it contains a ♯4 and major 7, and is considered by many jazz players as another maj7+ mode. The first interval, however, is a ♯2 and along with the ♯4 degree can produce exotic and bluesy sounds; however, the addition of the ♯5 create more of a Lydian augmented sound. This mode creates unusual tension over a maj7 chord. You can simply hear why jazz players include this mode in their vocabulary. *(Please note that this is the third maj7+ mode that we've encountered; unfortunately, these scales have not been categorized accurately in the past. It is important to keep in mind the scale of origin in order to play the correct notes that make up each mode).*

Mode: HMaj Mode 6
Formula: 1 ♯2 3 ♯4 ♯5 6 7 8
Construction: m3 H W W H W H
Chord Types: maj7+
Diatonic Harmony: Imaj7+, ♯II°7, IIImaj7 add♭13, ♯IVm7♭5, ♯V7♯9, VIm(maj7)add♯11, VII7♭9
Key Signature: Add one sharp, or subtract one flat

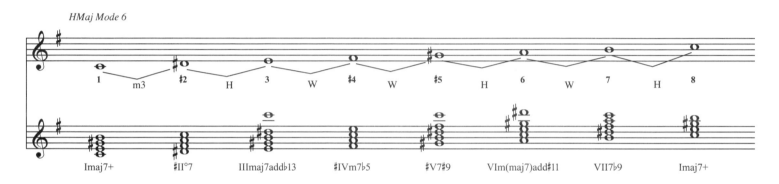

HMaj Mode 7 has limited use other than providing another option over diminished chords. You can, however, create some interesting sounds using this mode over a dominant chord (or, as we have previously discussed, an altered dominant chord).

Mode: HMaj Mode 7
Formula: 1 ♭2(♭9) ♭3(♯9) 4 ♭5(♯11) ♭6(♭13) ♭♭7 8
Construction: H W W H W H m3
Chord Types: °7
Diatonic Harmony: I°7, ♭IImaj7 add♭13, ♭IIIm7♭5, IV7♯9, ♭Vm(maj7)add♯11, ♭VI7♭9, ♭♭VIImaj7+
Key Signature: Add five flats, or subtract five sharps

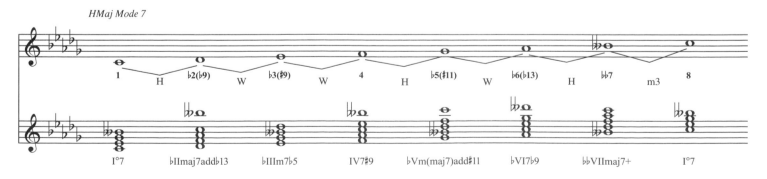

Scale of origin: Tonal Pentatonic Scales

You first learn some of the basic material like improvising with pentatonic scales with added blue notes. But, afterwards, you just want to go and check it out in every possible way.
Mike Stern

A *tonal pentatonic scale* is a five-note scale that contains no half steps.

There is certainly more to pentatonic scales than simple box patterns and repeated blues riffs. These five-note scales offer a fountain of musical possibilities; unfortunately, many guitar players limit themselves to only looking at one or two scale shapes without also taking into account the harmonic colors found in patterns that we already have under our fingers.

The scales below are illustrated to provide you with a different way of looking at these familiar patterns. Notice that the chord type is generalized to include only a basic tonality: major, minor, or dominant. Although a specific chord choice has been made, the harmonic suggestions are just suggestions. Without getting into too much of a theoretical discussion that is beyond the scope of this book, we're basically applying the same modal approach used in the previous sections to pentatonic scales. Each of these scales implies some sort of harmonic color (or chord), and we've simply taken the liberty to explore these harmonies and suggest chord names. It is recommended that you do the same.

The diatonic harmony has been illustrated as a point of reference. You can hear them demonstrated on the accompanying CD.

Remember, your playing will sound the same unless you take a new look at what you've been doing. Originally these modes served simply as positions that mapped out the scale over the entire fretboard, but by applying the modal approach to these scales we can begin to see unlimited possibilities. Let's take a look at these modes one at a time.

TP Mode 1 is the popular *major pentatonic scale* and, as its name suggests, is derived from the major scale (or Ionian mode). Every guitarist should be familiar with this scale as it is often heard in country and rock music. Many folk melodies from different cultures are also based on this scale.

> Mode: TP Mode 1 Major Pentatonic
> Formula: 1 2 3 5 6 8
> Construction: W W m3 W m3
> Chord Types: major
> Diatonic Harmony: I6, II7sus4, IIIm7+, Vsus4, VIm7
> Key Signature: No sharps or flats (for the key of C)

TP Mode 1

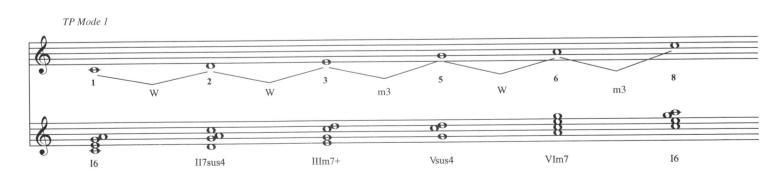

TP Mode 2 begins on the second degree of the major pentatonic scale. This scale occurs in "old-timey" folk music of the American Southeast. Contemporary bluegrass and country musicians use this mode to create a haunting, traditional sound.

Mode: TP Mode 2
Formula: 1 2 4 5 ♭7 8
Construction: W m3 W m3 W
Chord Types: dominant
Diatonic Harmony: I7sus4, IIm7+, IVsus4, Vm7, ♭VII6
Key Signature: Add one flat, or subtract one sharp

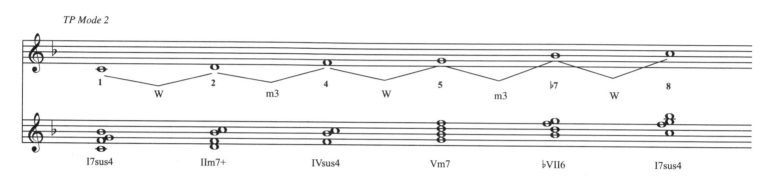

TP Mode 3 begins on the third degree of the major pentatonic scale. Because of its ambiguous tonal center, this mode has limited use.

Mode: TP Mode 3
Formula: 1 ♭3 4 ♭6 ♭7 8
Construction: m3 W m3 W W
Chord Types: minor
Diatonic Harmony: Im7+, ♭IIIsus4, IVm7, ♭VI6, ♭VII7sus4
Key Signature: Add three flats, or subtract three sharps

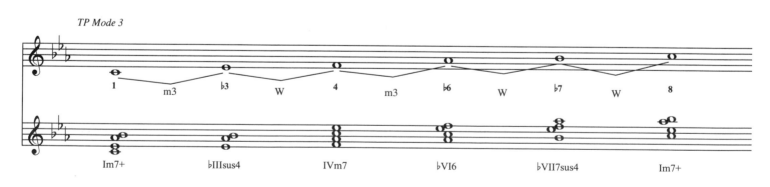

TP Mode 4 begins on the fourth degree of the major pentatonic scale. This mode is sometimes considered the "true" tonal pentatonic scale. It occurs in ancient music around the globe, but has limited use in usual contemporary settings. However, it can be heard in avant-garde, new age, and "world" musics that reflect African, Asian, or Celtic influences.

Mode: TP Mode 4
Formula: 1 2 4 5 6 8
Construction: W m3 W W m3
Chord Types: dominant
Diatonic Harmony: Isus4, IIm7, IV6, V7sus4, VIm7+
Key Signature: Add one flat, or subtract one sharp

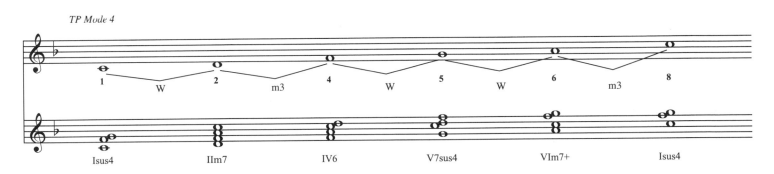

TP Mode 5 begins on the fifth degree of the major pentatonic scale. This mode is also known as the *minor pentatonic scale* and can be considered tonal pentatonic minor mode 1; however, the scale formulas and diatonic harmonies would not change. TP Mode 5 is the relative minor of TP Mode 1 and is the basis for blues music and, of course, blues-based rock and jazz. This mode contains the same notes as the Dorian, Phrygian, and Aeolian modes and is sometimes combined with these modes to create interesting melodies.

Mode: TP Mode 5 (Minor Pentatonic Mode 1)
Formula: 1 ♭3 4 5 ♭7 8
Construction: m3 W W m3 W
Chord Types: minor
Diatonic Harmony: Im7, ♭III6, IV7sus4, Vm7+, ♭VIIsus4
Key Signature: Add three flats, or subtract three sharps

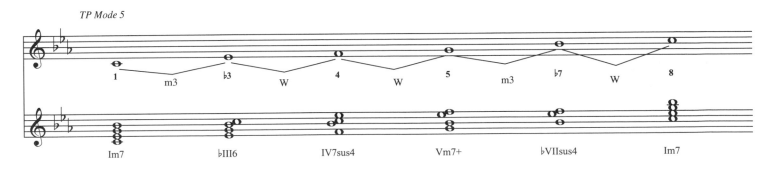

Scale of origin: Semitonal Pentatonic Scale Type 1

A *semitonal pentatonic scale* is a five-note scale that includes half steps. There are technically two such scales and will be referred to as Type 1 and Type 2 respectfully. Semitonal Pentatonic Type 1 is created by omitting scale degrees 2 and 6 from the major scale; while Semitonal Pentatonic Type 2 omits scale degrees 2 and 5 (also from the major scale).

Generally speaking, semitonal pentatonic scales add a strong dissonant flavor to improvisational lines and melodies. These unusual scales (and their respective modes) are usually associated with the musics of specific cultures. For this reason the harmonic analysis serves as a general reference. Additionally, some of the ethnic scales (discussed later in this book) may also be viewed as semitonal pentatonics.

SP Type 1 Mode 1 is built on the first degree of the semitonal pentatonic scale and can also be viewed Cmaj7add11 arpeggio. This scale has a strong Ionian sound and works well over a major tonality. (*Note:* Sometimes all it takes is avoiding certain notes and these limitations can lead to the creation of new ideas. SP Type 1 Mode 1 is a perfect example of this.)

Mode: SP Type 1 Mode 1 (C major no 2 & no 6)
Formula: 1 3 4 5 7 8
Construction: M3 H W M3 H
Chord Types: major
Diatonic Harmony: Imaj7, IIIm add♭6, IVmaj7♯11(no 3), V7(no 5), VIIsus4♭5
Key Signature: No sharps or flats (for the key of C)

SP Type 1 Mode 1

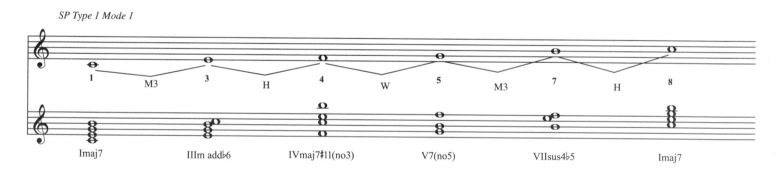

SP Type 1 Mode 2 is built on the second degree of the semitonal pentatonic scale and/or the third degree of the major scale. This mode has strong Phrygian properties and, subsequently, an exotic minor sound.

Mode: SP Type 1 Mode 2
Formula: 1 ♭2 ♭3 5 ♭6 8
Construction: H W M3 H M3
Chord Types: minor
Diatonic Harmony: Im add♭6, ♭IImaj7♯11(no 3), ♭III7(no 5), Vsus4♭5, ♭VImaj7
Key Signature: Add four flats, or subtract four sharps

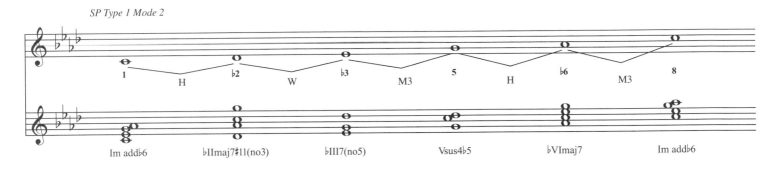

SP Type 1 Mode 3 is built on the third degree of the semitonal pentatonic scale and/or the fourth degree of the major scale and, just like its scale of origin, the strong Lydian sound works well at creating tension over a maj7 tonality.

Mode: SP Type 1 Mode 3
Formula: 1 2 ♯4 5 7 8
Construction: W M3 H M3 H
Chord Types: major
Diatonic Harmony: Imaj7♯11(no 3), II7(no 5), ♯IVsus4♭5, Vmaj7, VIIm add♭6
Key Signature: Add one sharp, or subtract one flat

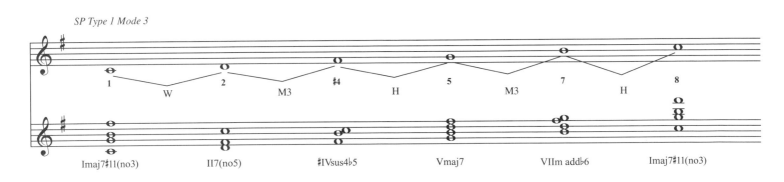

SP Type 1 Mode 4 is built on the fourth degree of the semitonal pentatonic scale. By now you should have noticed the pattern, SP Type 1 Mode 4 is built on the fifth degree of the major scale, therefore, its mother scale is Mixolydian. And as we already know, any scale with Mixolydian properties works well over dominant chords.

Mode: SP Type 1 Mode 4
Formula: 1 3 4 6 ♭7 8
Construction: M3 H M3 H W
Chord Types: dominant
Diatonic Harmony: I7(no 5), IIIsus4♭5, IVmaj7, VIm add♭6, ♭VIImaj7♯11(no 3)
Key Signature: Add one flat, or subtract one sharp

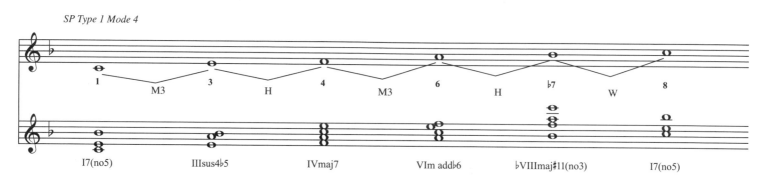

SP Type 1 Mode 5 is built on the fifth degree of the semitonal pentatonic scale and/or the seventh degree of the major scale. Yeah, you guessed it—Locrian. This mode works well for altered or altering dominant chords.

Mode: SP Type 1 Mode 5
Formula: 1 ♭2 4 ♭5 ♭6 8
Construction: H M3 H W M3
Chord Types: dominant
Diatonic Harmony: Isus4♭5, ♭IImaj7, IVm add♭6, ♭Vmaj7♯11(no 3), ♭VI7(no 5)
Key Signature: Add five flats, or subtract five sharps

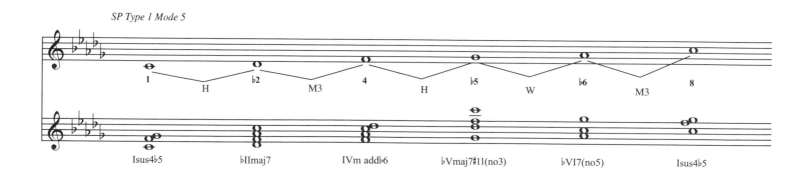

Scale of origin: Semitonal Pentatonic Scale Type 2

SP Type 2 Mode 1 is the Ionian mode without the second and fifth degrees. This mode offers another option for playing over major chords.

> Mode: SP Type 2 Mode 1 (C major no 2 & no 5)
> Formula: 1 3 4 6 7 8
> Construction: M3 H M3 W H
> Chord Types: major
> Diatonic Harmony: Imaj7(no5), IIIsus4, IVmaj7, VIm, VII7♭5sus4
> Key Signature: No sharps or flats (for the key of C)

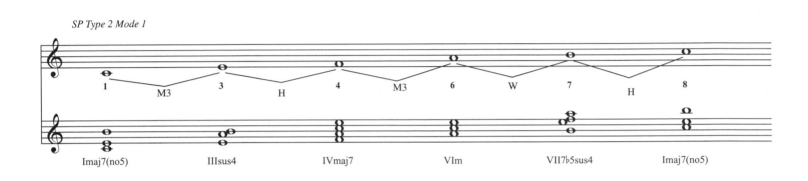

SP Type 2 Mode 2 is built on the third degree of the major scale. The tonality is somewhat ambiguous due to the lack of the third and seventh degrees; however, the ♭2 creates a hint of the Phrygian sound. Notice the exotic flavor created by the major third intervals between ♭2 and 4, and ♭6 and 8.

> Mode: SP Type 2 Mode 2
> Formula: 1 ♭2 4 5 ♭6 8
> Construction: H M3 W H M3
> Chord Types: dominant
> Diatonic Harmony: Isus4, ♭IImaj7, IVm, V7♭5sus4, ♭VImaj7(no5)
> Key Signature: Add four flats, or subtract four sharps

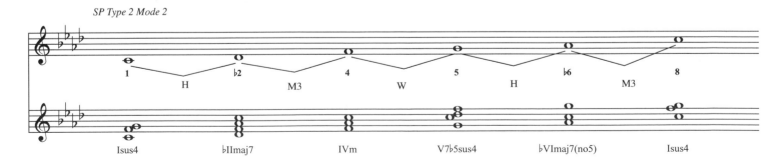

SP Type 2 Mode 3 is built on the fourth degree of the major scale and, as we have seen in the previous examples, has properties that resemble the Lydian mode. The third and leading tone provide a strong major tonality while the raised fourth creates that characteristic Lydian sound.

> Mode: SP Type 2 Mode 3
> Formula: 1 3 ♯4 5 7 8
> Construction: M3 W H M3 H
> Chord Types: major
> Diatonic Harmony: Imaj7, IIIm, ♯IV7♭5sus4, Vmaj7(no5), VIIsus4
> Key Signature: Add one sharp, or subtract one flat

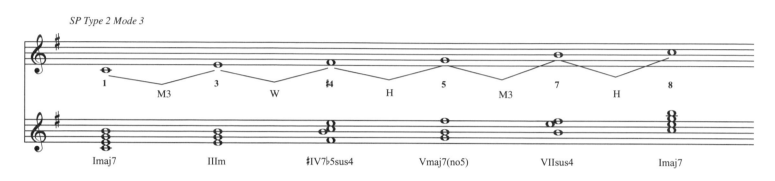

SP Type 2 Mode 4 is built on the sixth degree of the major scale and has an Aeolian sound. This mode creates a dark atmosphere that almost sounds diminished.

> Mode: SP Type 2 Mode 4
> Formula: 1 2 ♭3 5 ♭6 8
> Construction: W H M3 H M3
> Chord Types: minor
> Diatonic Harmony: Im, II7♭5sus4, ♭IIImaj7(no5), Vsus4, ♭VImaj7
> Key Signature: Add three flats, or subtract three sharps

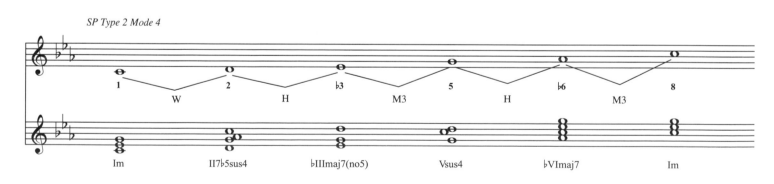

SP Type 2 Mode 5 is built on the seventh degree of the major scale. Although this mode contains Locrian properties, the absence of the minor third make this scale available for creating dark and sinister melodies over dominant chords.

Mode: SP Type 2 Mode 5
Formula: 1 ♭2 4 ♭5 ♭7 8
Construction: H M3 H W M3
Chord Types: dominant
Diatonic Harmony: I7♭5sus4, ♭IImaj7(no5), IVsus4, ♭Vmaj7, ♭VIIm
Key Signature: Add five flats, or subtract five sharps

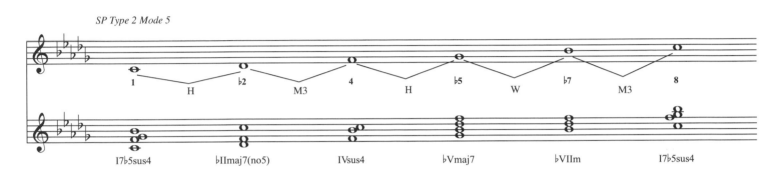

In short, this section on semitonal pentatonic scales provides ideas that create, what I like to refer to as, "modal pentatonics." The concept simply being that we can create modal sounds that add different colors to the harmony while using the five-note scale patterns that we, as guitar players, have grown so accustomed to. There is a certain symmetry to pentatonic scales that have made them a favorite among guitarists and these modal pentatonics can provide you with new ideas and sounds that will expand your vocabulary.

The Relative Approach

The bottom line is how it sounds.
Steve Vai

Let's apply the modes that we've just discussed to a real playing situation.

The purpose of the relative approach is to help you understand the scale-within-a-scale concept that is the basis for modal theory. By making each scale degree the tonic you are changing the tonality of the scale and thereby creating different possibilities for its application. For example, you may play a C major scale over a D minor chord and create a Dorian sound, but if you think in terms of creating a D Dorian scale to play over a D minor chord you will be capturing the essence of the mode rather the playing a game of connect-the-dots. This will become clearer as you play the following examples.

For the benefit of those who skipped the "How to Use This Book" section, we will define what is meant by the relative approach. Notice in the example below that the notes from the C major (or Ionian) scale are the same notes as those in the A minor (or Aeolian) scale. The notes themselves are the same (that is, no sharps or flats); however, the scales begin and end on different notes. Therefore, the C major scale is said to be the relative major of A minor, and likewise, the A minor is said to be the relative minor of C major.

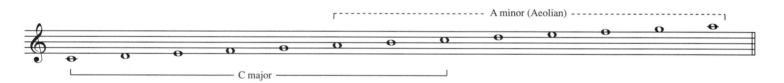

Let's take a look at the two more examples:

In the first example, C Ionian is said to be the relative Ionian of D Dorian and D Dorian is the relative Dorian of C Ionian. When two different scales are made up of the same notes (and share the same key signature) they are said to be relative (or related) to each other.

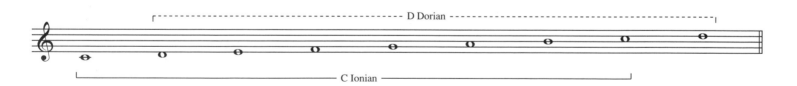

And in the second example, C Ionian is said to be the relative Ionian of E Phrygian and E Phrygian is the relative Phrygian of C Ionian.

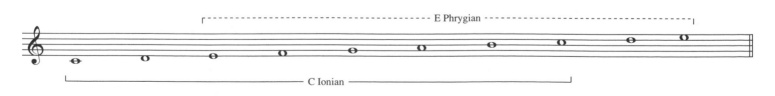

Major Modes

The chord chart below will guide you through the music example. Notice that the diatonic harmony is the same as the diatonic harmony for the Ionian mode.

Jazz Minor Modes

Let's take a look at the modes created from the jazz minor scale...

Harmonic Minor Modes

Now, let's try the modes from the harmonic minor scale…

Harmonic Major Modes

Let's check out the modes created from the harmonic major scale (I'll bet your jazz buddies will be envious)…

Tonal Pentatonic Modes

Now we'll try the relative approach with the modes created from the tonal pentatonic scale.

Semitonal Pentatonic Type 1 Modes

The semitonals may take a little getting used to...

Semitonal Pentatonic Type 2 Modes

And finally, the modes created from the semitonal pentatonic type 2 scale...

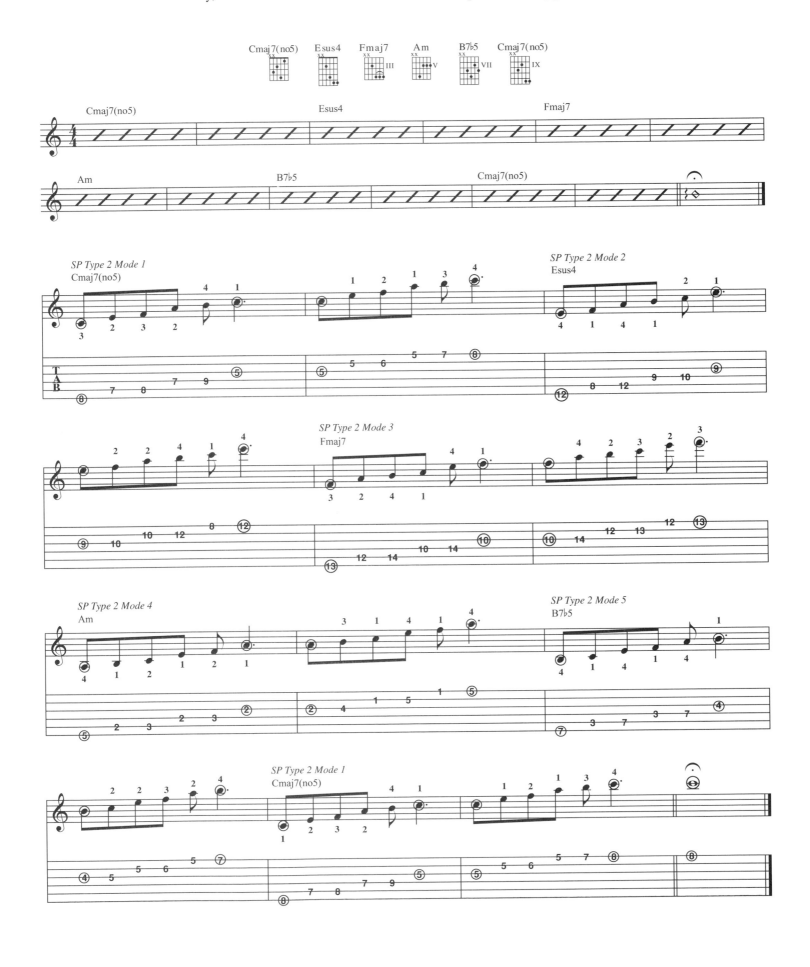

The Parallel Approach

The scale or the chord or the technique, in itself, is nothing until you internalize it and throw it back in a musical way. By that point, you have forgotten where you got it. You are using it in a sentence or a word or a conversation.
John Scofield

The parallel approach simply means that you build all of the scales off of the same note—in this case, C. The purpose of this approach is to help you familiarize yourself with the modes by listening for the differences between them. In the relative approach your ears sometimes fool you into thinking that you are hearing the mode when in actuality you are basically hearing scale patterns. By exploring the modes in this fashion you will train your fingers, ears, and mind to think modally; that is, in terms of sounds and not finger patterns.

The parallel approach forces you to think outside of the box as you make subtle alterations to fit the appropriate mode over its underlying harmony.

Let's take a look at the two examples:

In the example below, C Ionian is parallel to C Dorian and C Dorian is parallel to C Ionian. Again, when different scales share the same tonic they are said to be parallel with each other. Notice that the key signature changes.

And in the second example, C Ionian is parallel to C Phrygian and C Phrygian is parallel to C Ionian...

(16) (17) Major Modes

The chord chart below will guide you through the music example. Notice that the diatonic harmony is the same as the diatonic harmony for the Ionian mode except that every chord is essentially the I chord.

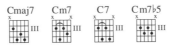

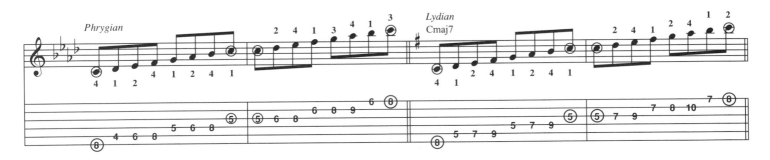

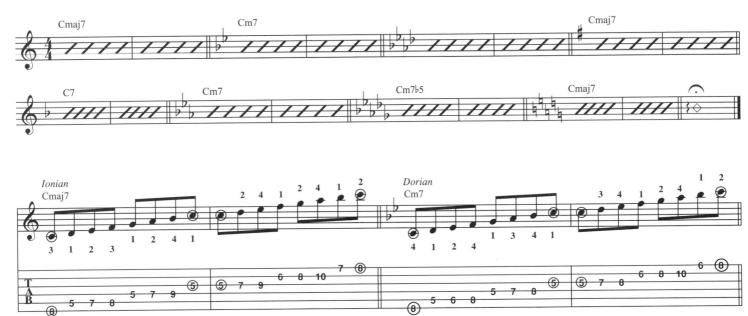

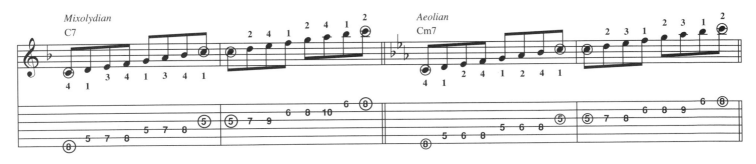

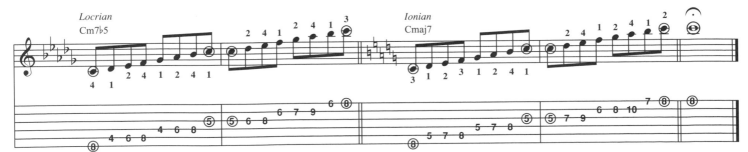

Jazz Minor Modes

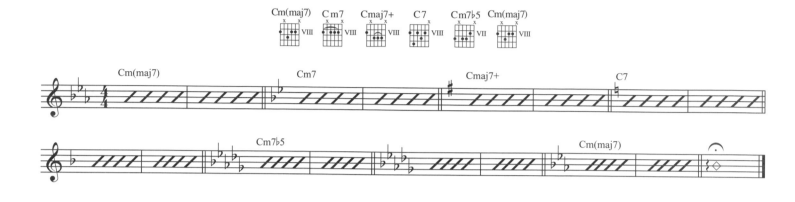

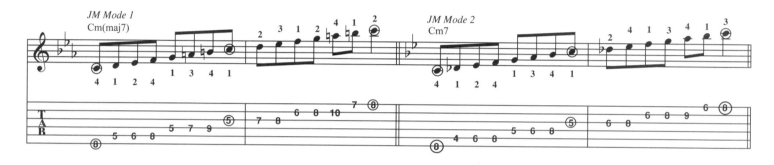

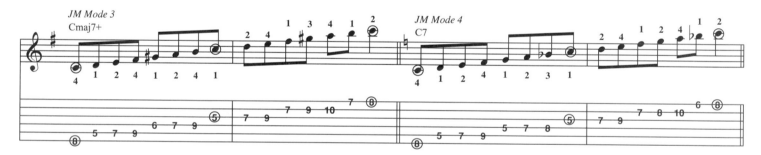

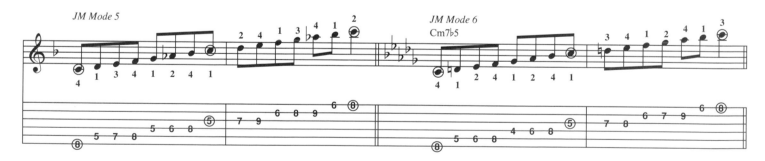

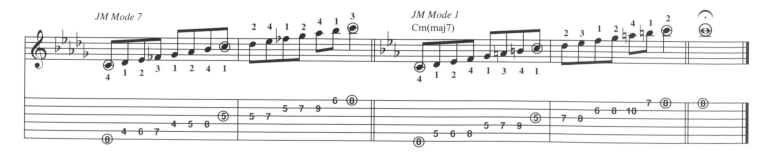

Harmonic Minor Modes

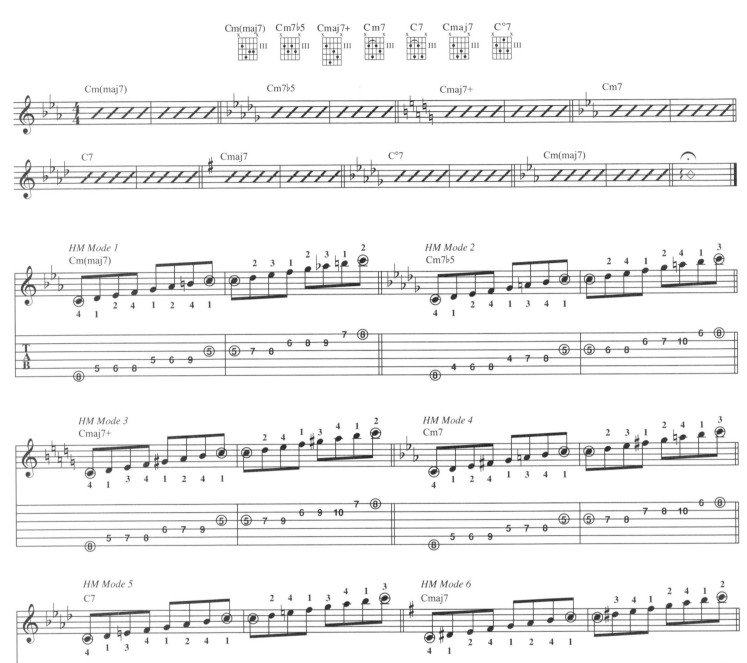

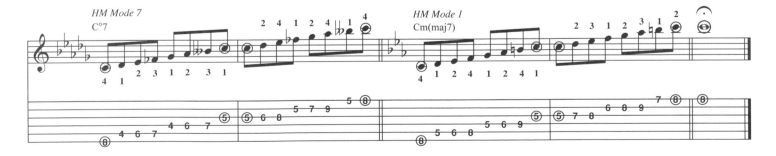

Harmonic Major Modes

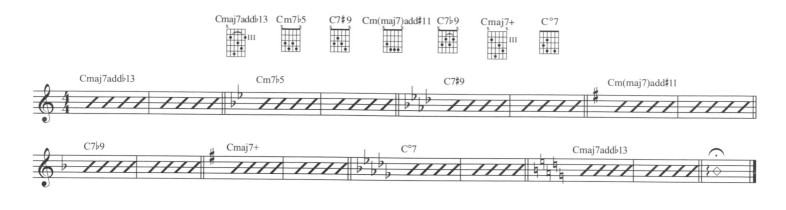

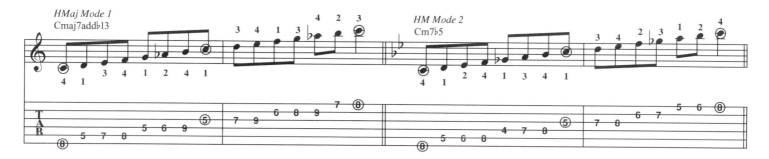

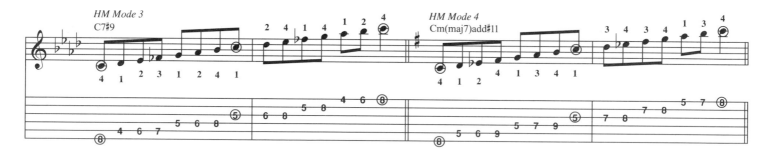

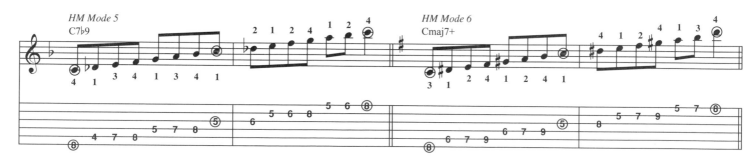

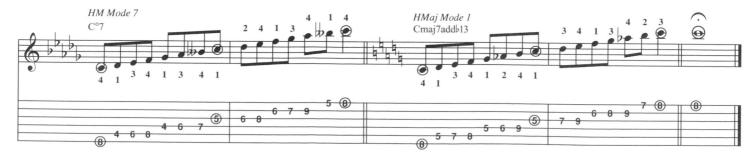

Tonal Pentatonic Modes

Semitonal Pentatonic Type 1 Modes

Semitonal Pentatonic Type 2 Modes

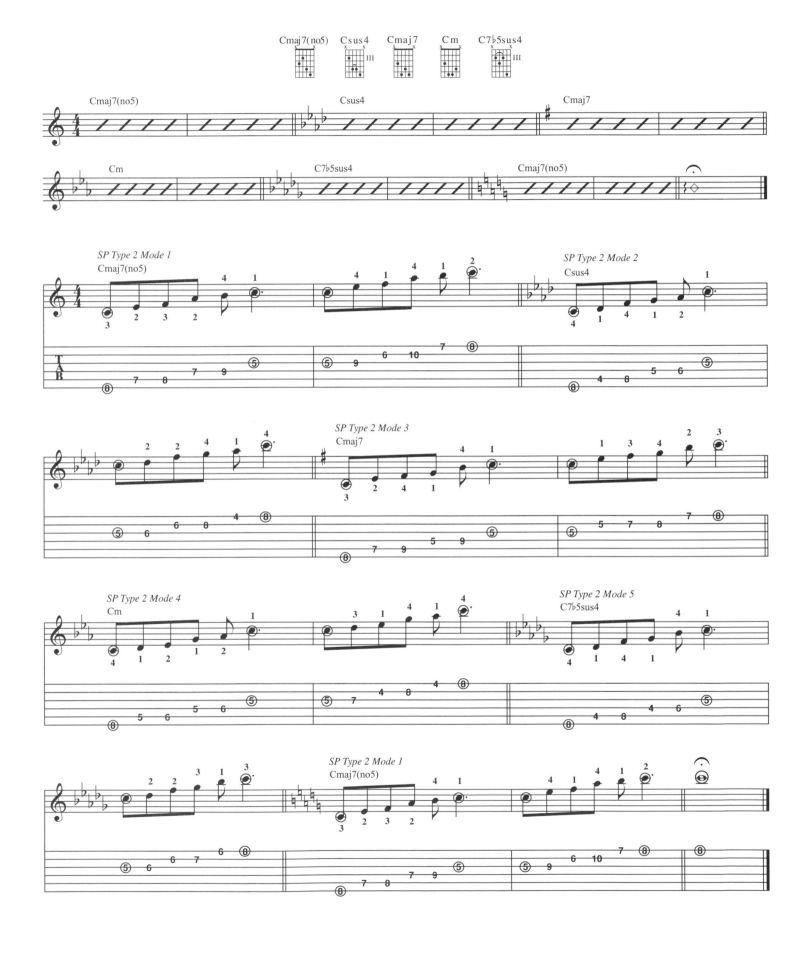

Advanced Scales

I had been studying with Jim Hall… and just wanted to play bebop. I couldn't see anything else. Then something snapped and I realized that I had cut myself off from all of the music that had led me to that point.
Bill Frisell

The following scales are included for the advancing guitarist. These scales provide the improviser with many different options for creating melodies. Stylistically you'll find these scales performed by jazz, progressive-rock, and modern-blues players alike. Those of you that have an enterprising nature may wish to explore these scales using the same modal approaches that we have previously discussed.

Your imagination is the only limitation. Try building a mode for each scale degree and you'll discover different sounds that will spark your creativity. Although these scales are also used compositionally, they are prominent among improvisers and provide a wealth of ideas that make up an instrumentalist's vocabulary. Let's begin by looking at the blues scales.

Author's note: There is no hard-and-fast rule for key signature application with regard to the following advanced and ethnic scales. In most cases the respective parallel major or minor is used. For this reason we will leave out the key signature formula. Also notice that the diatonic harmony has been omitted. There are too many possibilities to discuss and these scales are simply not used in that fashion.

There are three types of blues scales below: major, minor, and dominant. Each of these scales adds a blues quality to the aforementioned tonalities. This is accomplished by adding "blue notes" to an already familiar scale.

Blue notes are those notes (or scale degrees) that provide the blues sound to a scale, arpeggio, or chord. They are the notes that sound hip. The blue notes are scale degrees ♭3 (or ♯9), ♭5, and ♭7; or, in the key of C, notes E♭, G♭, and B♭.

Blues Scale Type 1 is simply a major pentatonic scale with an added ♭3 scale degree. This scale is also known as the *"major" six-note blues scale* and works at adding a bluesy sound to major chords.

> Scale: Blues Scale Type 1 ("Major" Six-Note Blues Scale)
> Formula: 1 2 ♭3 ♮3 5 6 8
> Construction: W H H m3 W m3
> Chord Types: 6add♯9, major

Blues Scale Type 1 ("Major" Six-Note Blues Scale)

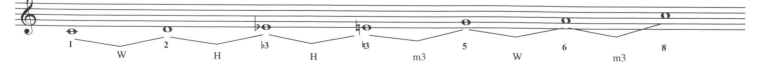

Blues Scale Type 1 ("Major" Six-Note Blues Scale)

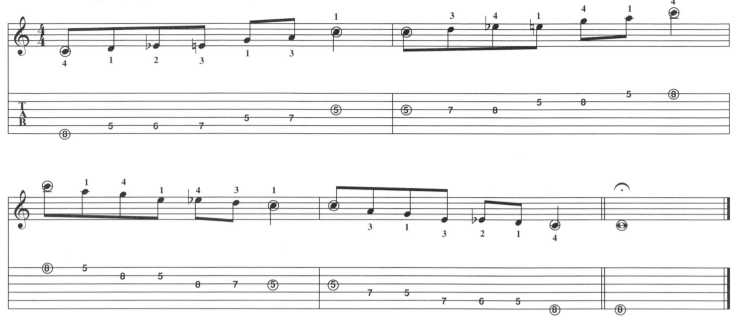

Blues Scale Type 2 ("Minor" Six-Note Blues Scale)

Blues Scale Type 2 is simply a minor pentatonic scale with an added ♭5 scale degree. This scale is also known as the *"minor" six-note blues scale* and works at adding a bluesy sound to minor chords. Many guitarists have also used this scale successfully over dominant chords. (*Author's note:* This scale has also been inappropriately called the pentatonic blues scale. It is inappropriate because it contains six notes thereby making it a *hexatonic* scale.)

Scale: Blues Scale Type 2 ("Minor" Six-Note Blues Scale)
Formula: 1 ♭3 4 ♭5 ♮5 ♭7 8
Construction: m3 W H H m3 W
Chord Types: m11, minor, dominant

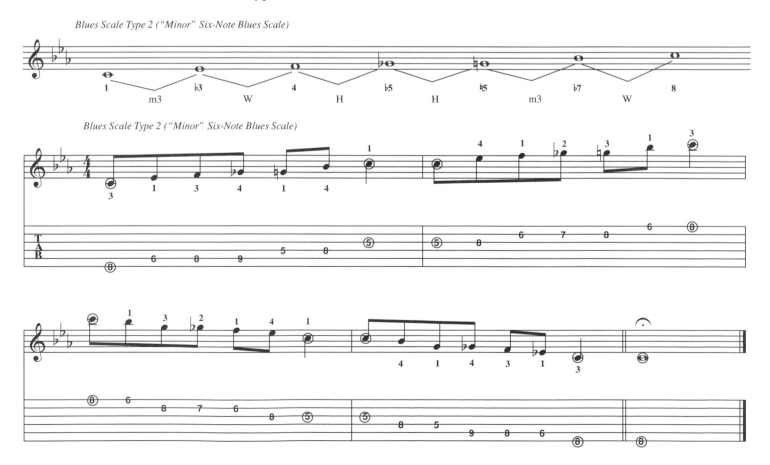

Blues Scale Type 3 is simply a minor pentatonic scale with added ♮3 and ♭5 scale degrees. This scale is also known as "the" blues scale and works at creating bluesy sounds over dominant chords.

Scale: Blues Scale Type 3 (Seven-Note Blues Scale)
Formula: 1 ♭3 ♮3 4 ♭5 ♮5 ♭7 8
Construction: m3 H H H H m3 W
Chord Types: 7♭5♯9, dominant

Blues Scale Type 3 (Seven-Note Blues Scale)

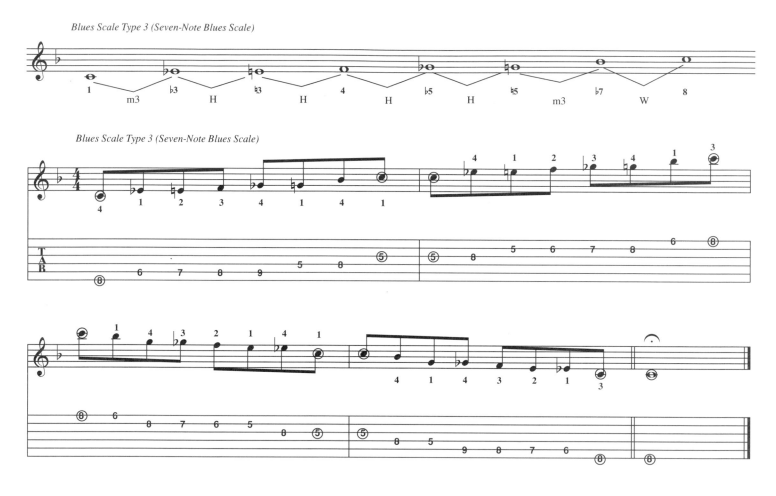

Blues Scale Type 3 (Seven-Note Blues Scale)

The **whole tone scale** is named as such because it is solely constructed using whole steps. This construction makes this scale very symmetrical; that is, you can begin this scale on any degree and still end up with the same scale (there aren't any possible modes). This scale works well for creating an augmented dominant sound.

Scale: Whole Tone
Formula: 1 2 3 ♯4(♯11) ♯5 ♭7 8
Construction: W W W W W W
Chord Types: 7+, dominant

Whole Tone Scale

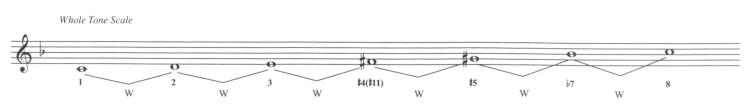

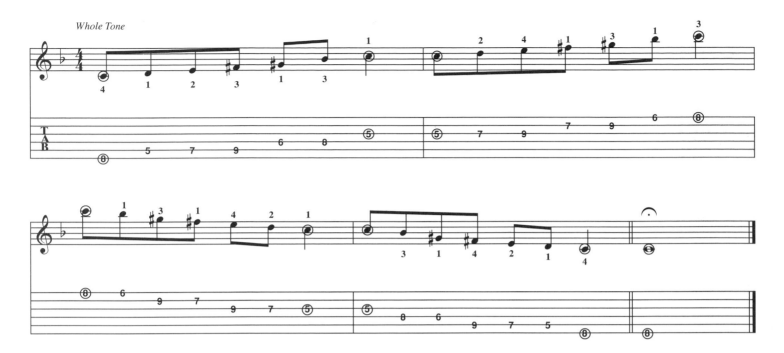

Whole Tone

The next two scales are also symmetrical. These, however, are diminished. Although **sym-metrical diminished type 1** is a "diminished" scale and is noted here with a m(maj7) tonality it is more often used for adding altered sounds to dominant chords. The 7 scale degree is simply used as a passing tone in such cases.

Scale: Symmetrical Diminished Type 1
Formula: 1 2 ♭3(♯9) 4 ♭5(♯11) ♭6(♭13) 6 7 8
Construction: W H W H W H W H
Chord Types: m(maj7), dominant

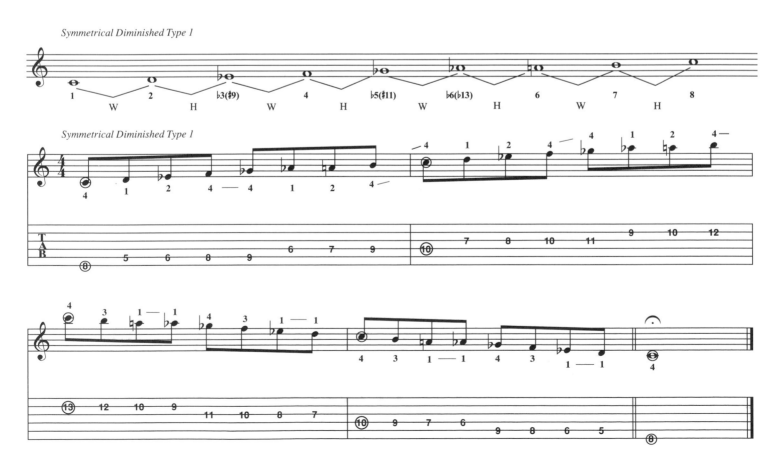

Symmetrical Diminished Type 1

Of the two types of symmetrical diminished scales, the ***symmetrical diminished type 2*** is the more popular one. Simply because of the hip colors created by the altered tensions (or chord extensions; *e.g.*, 9, 11, and 13). This scale includes the following altered tensions: ♭9, ♯9, and ♯11 (or ♭5). Notice that both of these scales can share the same fingering, simply move up (or down) one fret and maintain the same fingering. You're now playing the other type of symmetrical diminished scale.

Scale: Symmetrical Diminished Type 2
Formula: 1 ♭2(♭9) ♭3(♯9) ♮3 ♯4(♯11) 5 6 ♭7 8
Construction: H W H W H W H W
Chord Types: 7alt, dominant

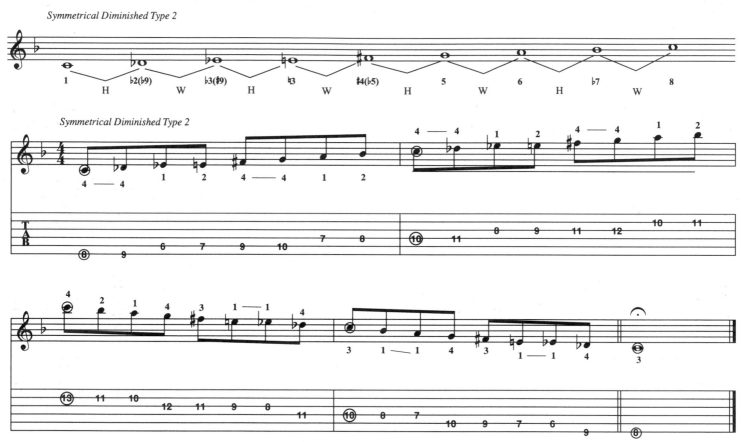

While still on the topic of symmetry we can discuss the final three advanced scales. The bebop scales were created by jazz players from the (you guessed it) Bebop era. These scales were developed to provide rhythmic symmetry. Beboppers are known for their improvisational flights taken at incredibly fast tempos. So by adding a passing tone to an Ionian, Dorian, or Mixolydian scale these players were able to play an eight-note scale and end it on the tonic and on the downbeat. You'll see this demonstrated below.

The *major bebop scale* is simply an Ionian scale with the ♯5 added as a passing tone and, as its name suggests, works well over major chords.

Scale: Major Bebop
Formula: 1 2 3 4 5 ♯5 6 7 8
Construction: W W H W H H W H
Chord Types: major

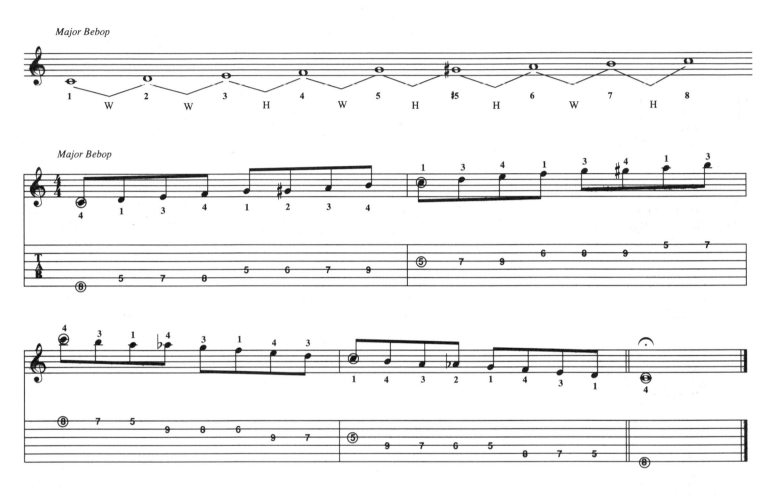

The *minor bebop scale* is simply a Dorian scale with the ♮3 added and works well over minor chords. Remember, at fast tempos the ♮3 will be heard as a passing tone and will not affect the overall minor tonality of the scale.

Scale: Minor Bebop
Formula: 1 2 ♭3 ♮3 4 5 6 ♭7 8
Construction: W H H H W W H W
Chord Types: minor

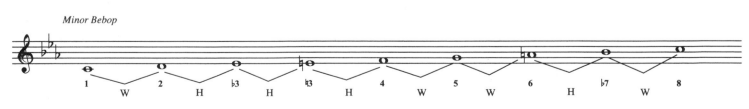

Minor Bebop

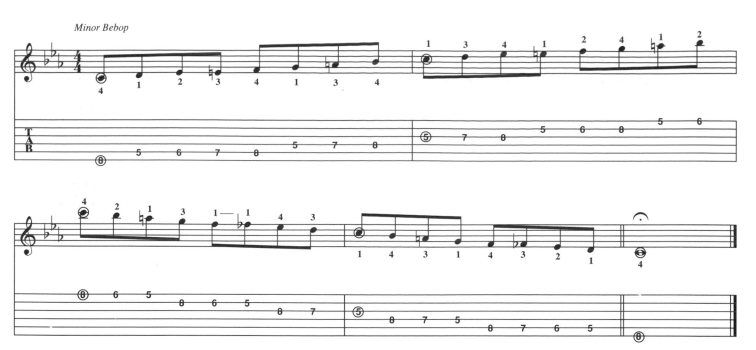

 The ***dominant bebop scale*** is simply a Mixolydian scale with the ♮7 added that also works as a passing tone. This is the most popular of the bebop scales.

Scale: Dominant Bebop
Formula: 1 2 3 4 5 6 ♭7 ♮7 8
Construction: W W H W W H H H
Chord Types: dominant

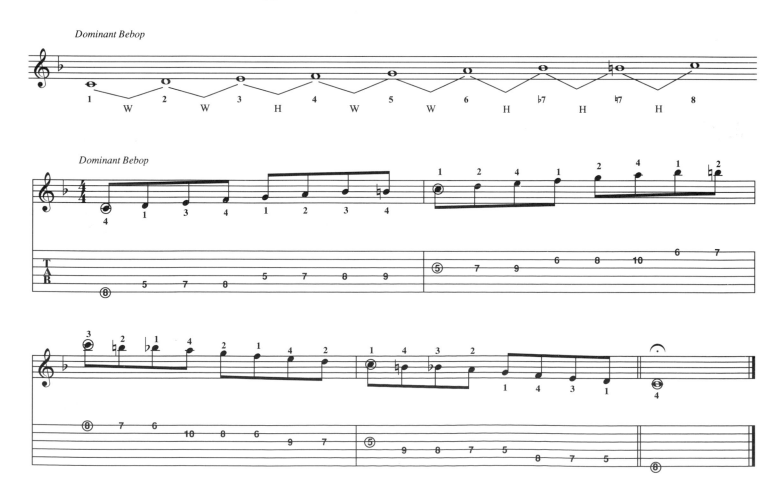

Dominant Bebop

Dominant Bebop

Ethnic Scales

Sometimes you have to research… I like things in the world music area, I usually look there for things that I haven't heard before.
Al Di Meola

Scales from other cultures have become a source of inspiration for many musicians and composers. We've already explored some of these sounds in the pentatonic section of this book. The following ethnic scales feature interesting "non-diatonic" harmonies. Some of these scales traditionally contained microtonal harmonies that have been interpreted for use with standard guitar tuning. Although you may find some of these scales inappropriate for traditional settings, they can be very effective for creating new age and world music style melodies.

Author's note: Diatonic harmony and key signature formulas have been omitted for reasons discussed in the previous section.

The **Gypsy minor scale** (also called *Hungarian minor*) features a ♭3 and ♭6 with a ♯4. It may also be viewed as a harmonic minor scale with a ♯4. This construction yields two minor third intervals that give this scale an immediately recognizable sound that is common in the folk music of Eastern Europe and contemporary music of Turkey and Israel. Béla Bartók and other composers devoted much attention to this scale and its applications in contemporary classical music.

Scale: Gypsy Minor (Hungarian Minor)
Formula: 1 2 ♭3 ♯4 5 ♭6 7 8
Construction: W H m3 H H m3 H
Chord Types: m(maj7)add♯11, minor

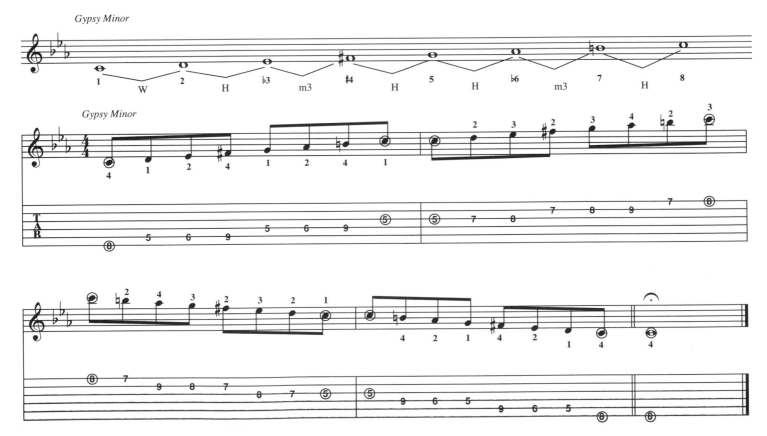

The ***Neapolitan minor scale*** features a ♭2, ♭3, and ♭6—and may also be viewed as a harmonic minor scale with a ♭2. This scale is identified with the *Neapolitan School*, a term loosely applied to an Italian style of composition popular in the 1700s.

Scale: Neapolitan Minor
Formula: 1 ♭2 ♭3 4 5 ♭6 7 8
Construction: H W W W H m3 H
Chord Types: m(maj7)add♭9, minor

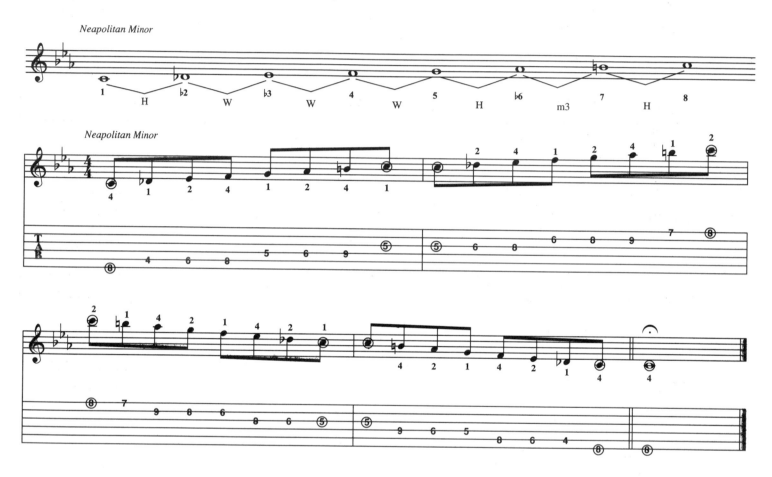

There is not much that can be said for the following scales. They have been included here for your consideration and for the sake of completeness. These scales are culture specific but can provide inspiration and creativity when applied to Western music.

Exploring these scales, as well as their respective modes, will take your playing into new directions and may provide the spark needed to break out of traditional sounding scales and arpeggios. World and new age musicians may find these scales to be an absolute necessity as they delve into more esoteric textures. With the exception of the Congolese and Indian scales, all of these scales may also be viewed as semitonal pentatonics.

Japanese Scales

Hirajoshi

Formula: 1 2 ♭3 5 ♭6 8
Construction: W H M3 H M3
Chord Types: m add♭6, minor

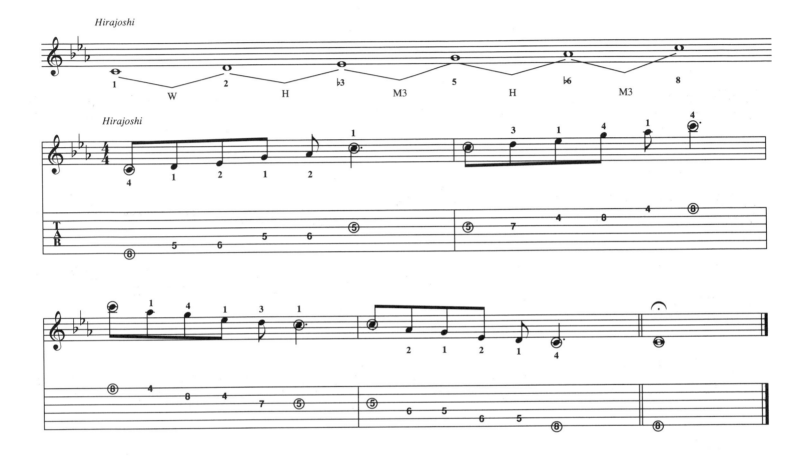

Kumoi

Formula: 1 2 ♭3 5 6 8

Construction: W H M3 W m3

Chord Types: m6, minor

In

Formula: 1 ♭2 4 5 ♭6 8
Construction: H M3 W H M3
Chord Types: sus4, dominant

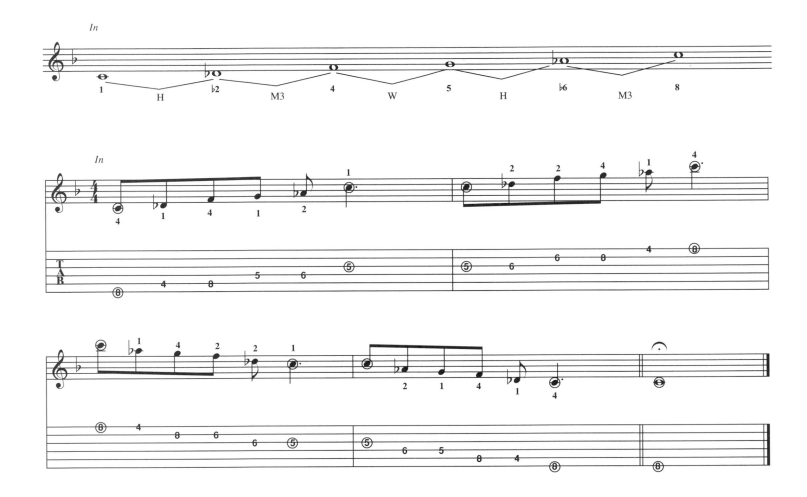

African Scales

Tanzanian

Formula: 1 2 ♭3 5 ♭7 8
Construction: W H M3 m3 W
Chord Types: m9, minor

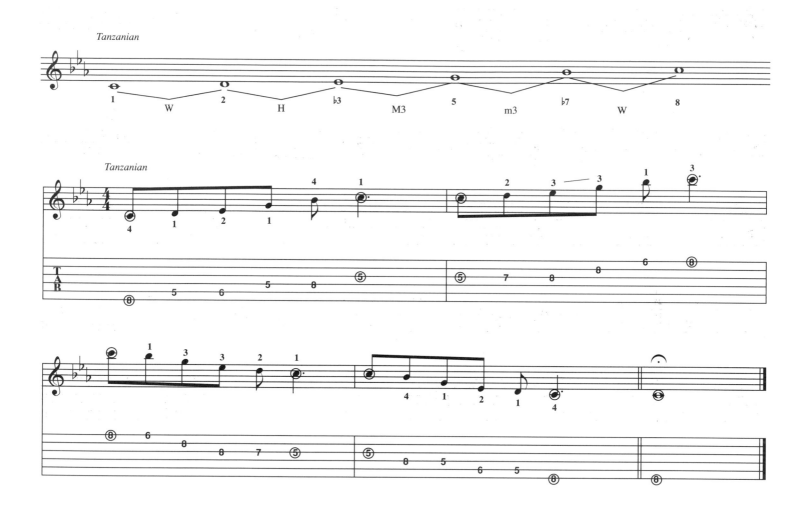

Congolese

Formula: 1 ♭3 ♭5 ♭6 ♭7 8
Construction: m3 m3 W W W
Chord Types: m7♭5add♭13, dominant

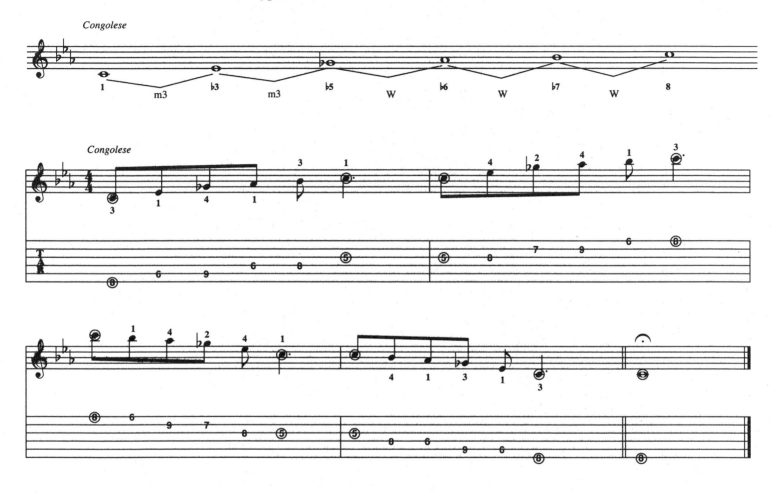

Indian Scales

Bhairava

Formula: 1 ♭2 3 4 5 ♭6 7 8

Construction: H m3 H W H m3 H

Chord Types: maj7, major

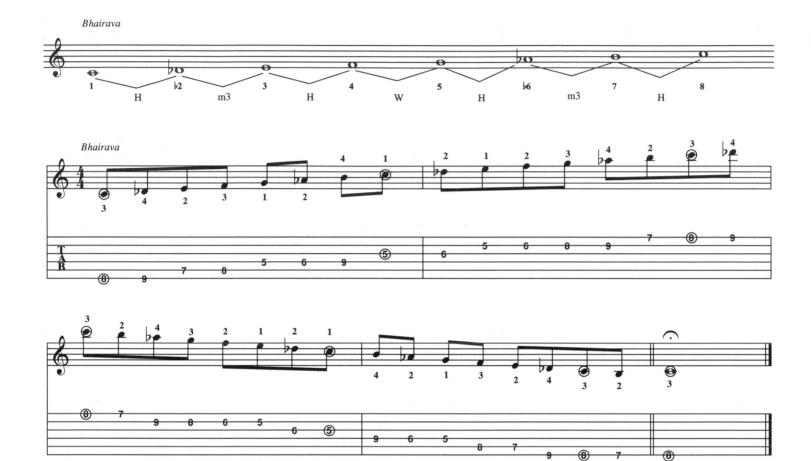

Pooravi

Formula: 1 ♭2 3 ♯4 5 ♭6 7 8

Construction: H m3 W H H m3 H

Chord Types: maj7♯11, major

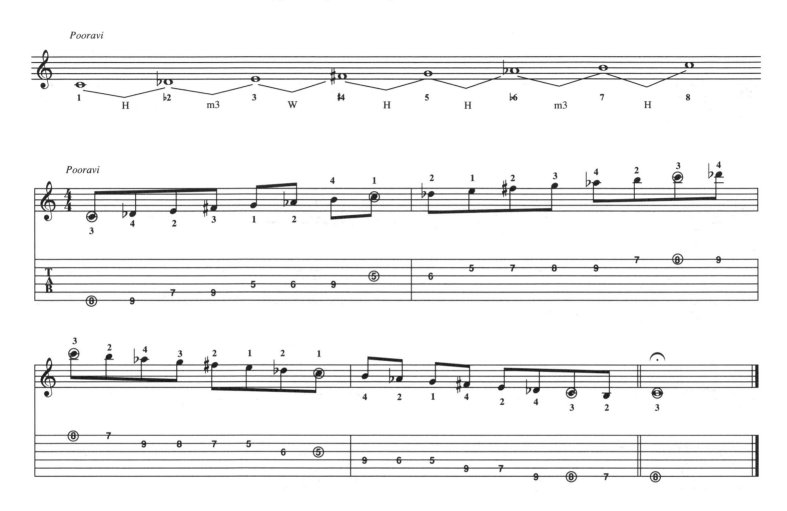

Marava

Formula: 1 ♭2 3 ♯4 5 6 7 8

Construction: H m3 W H W W H

Chord Types: maj7♯11, major

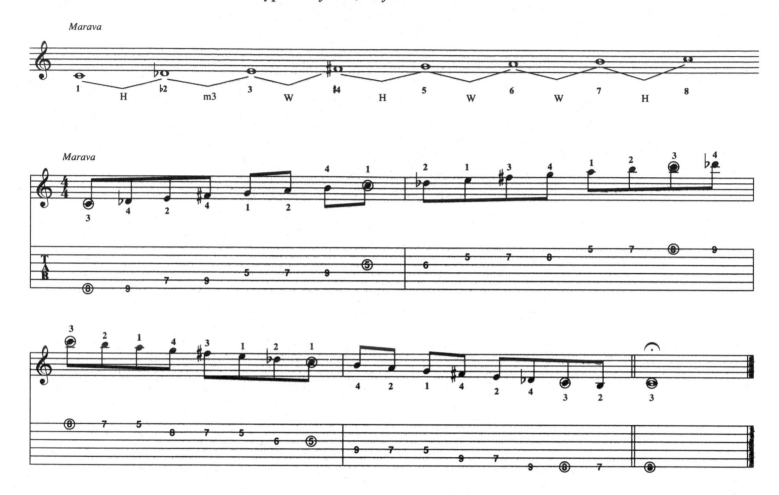

Kanakangi

Formula: 1 ♭2 ♭♭3 4 5 ♭6 ♭♭7 8
Construction: H H m3 W H W m3
Chord Types: sus4, dominant

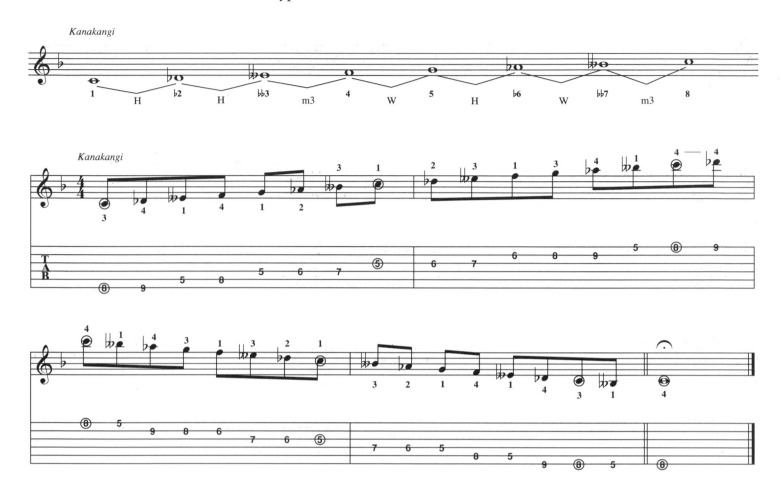

Balinese Scale

Pelog

Formula: 1 ♭2 ♭3 5 ♭6 8
Construction: H W M3 H M3
Chord Types: m add♭6, minor

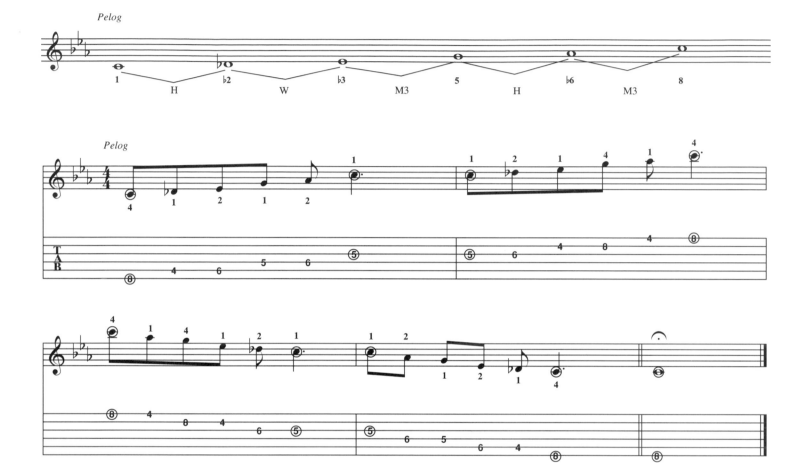

Modal Usage

It's all interpretation and sound...
Emily Remler

In this section all of the scales and modes that share the same tonality have been grouped together. They are presented here for your consideration. Please note that the implied tonality is represented by a chord symbol in parentheses. The CD track is included for practicing and developing new ideas. The backup band outlines the basic tonality (C, Cm, and C7 respectively) and you can create your own melodies using the available scales. You may wish to set the track to "repeat" so that you can explore each scale for as long as you like.

Some scales are available for both minor and dominant usage and, therefore, have been repeated in the subsequent sections.

Major Modes and Scales

This section contains all of the modes and scales available for use over a C major triad. Notice the slight alterations from one to the next.

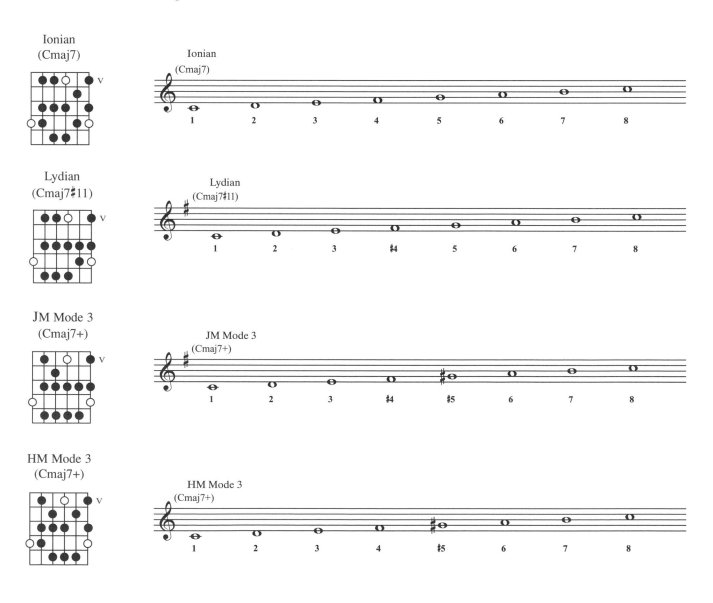

HM Mode 6
(Cmaj7)

HMaj Mode 1
(Cmaj7add♭13)

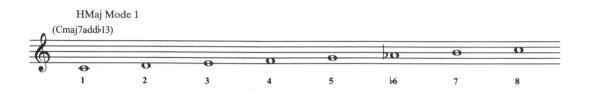

HMaj Mode 6
(Cmaj7+)

TP Mode 1
(C6)

SP Type 1 Mode 1
(Cmaj7)

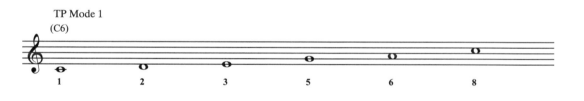

SP Type 1 Mode 3
(Cmaj7♯11[no3])

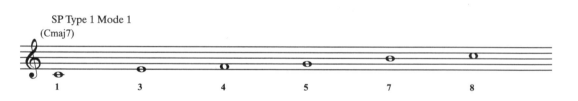

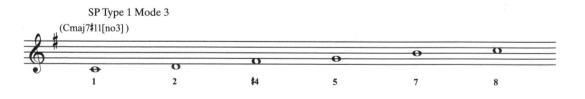

SP Type 2 Mode 1
(Cmaj7[no5])

SP Type 2 Mode 3
(Cmaj7)

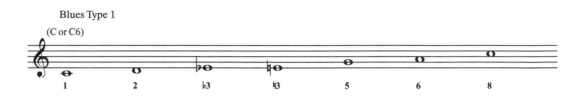

SP Type 2 Mode 3
(Cmaj7)

1   3   ♯4   5   7   8

Blues Type 1
(C or C6)

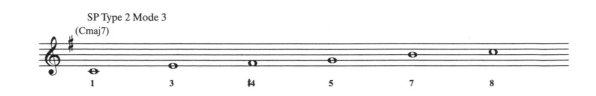

Blues Type 1

(C or C6)

1   2   ♭3   ♮3   5   6   8

Major Bebop
(Cmaj7)

Major Bebop
(Cmaj7)

1   2   3   4   5   ♯5   6   7   8

Bhairava
(Cmaj7)

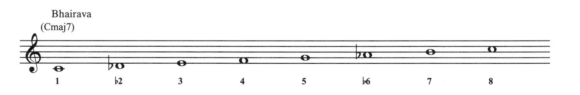

Bhairava
(Cmaj7)

1   ♭2   3   4   5   ♭6   7   8

Pooravi
(Cmaj7)

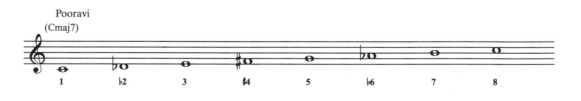

Pooravi
(Cmaj7)

1   ♭2   3   ♯4   5   ♭6   7   8

Marava
(Cmaj7)

Marava

1   ♭2   3   ♯4   5   6   7   8

73 Minor Modes and Scales

This section contains all of the modes available for use over minor chords. The backing band is vamping over a minor triad.

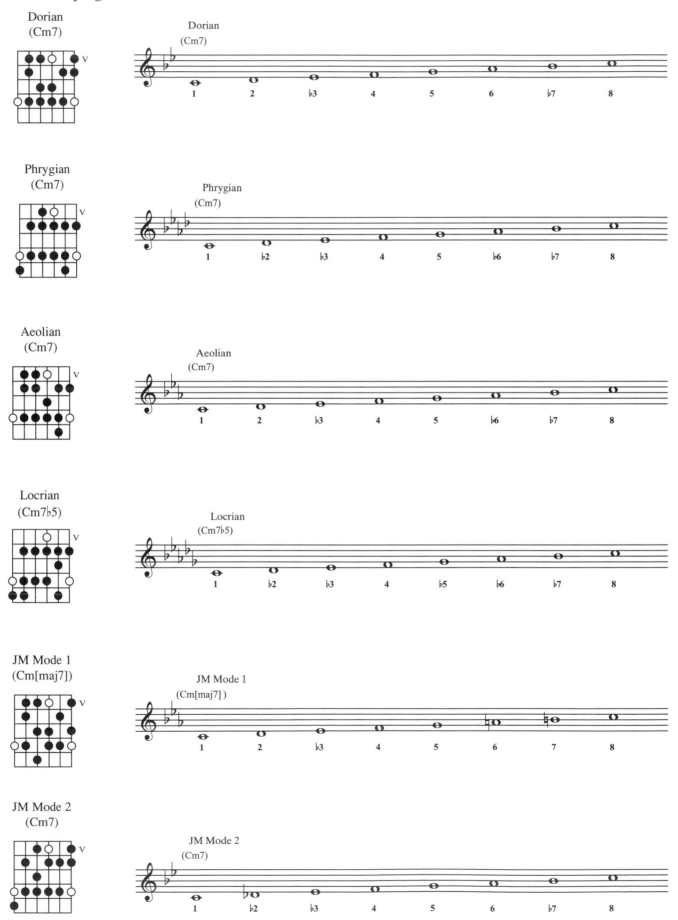

Dorian
(Cm7)

Phrygian
(Cm7)

Aeolian
(Cm7)

Locrian
(Cm7♭5)

JM Mode 1
(Cm[maj7])

JM Mode 2
(Cm7)

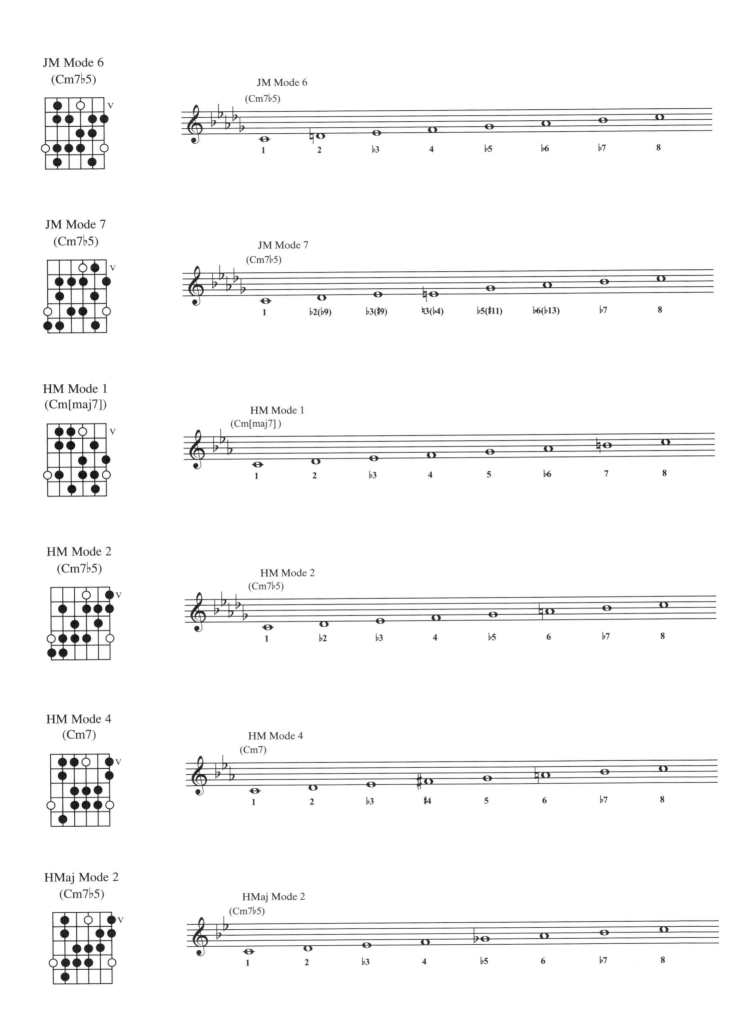

HMaj Mode 3
(Cm7)

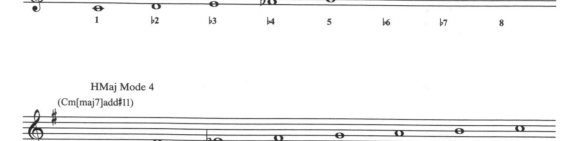

HMaj Mode 4
(Cm[maj7]add♯11)

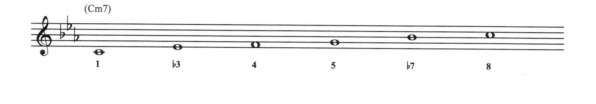

TP Mode 5
(Cm7)

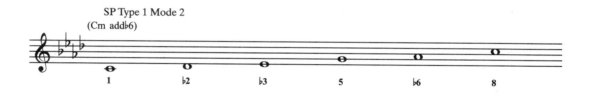

SP Type 1 Mode 2
(Cm add♭6)

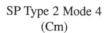

SP Type 2 Mode 4
(Cm)

Blues Type 2
(Cm7)

Minor Bebop
(Cm7)

Gypsy Minor
(Cm[maj7]add#11)

Neapolitan Minor
(Cm[maj7]add#11)

Hirajoshi
(Cm add♭6)

Kumoi
(Cm6)

Tanzanian
(Cm7)

Congolese
(Cm7♭5)

Pelog
(Cm)

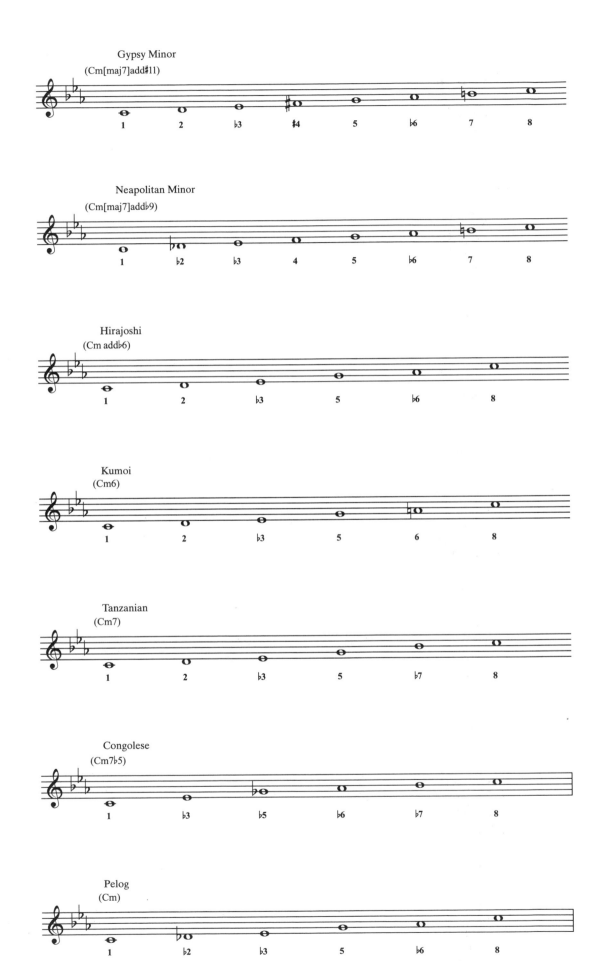

74 Dominant Modes and Scales

This section includes dominant scales and modes. The backing band is outlining a basic C7 tonality. You'll notice that some of the implied chord symbols indicate a C7alt. This is the symbol for an altered dominant chord.

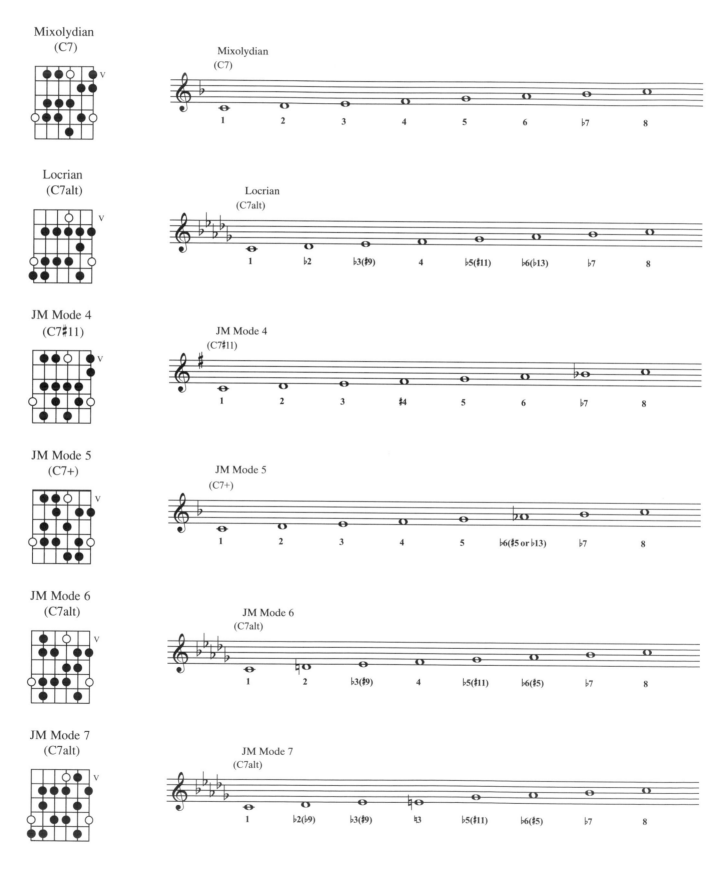

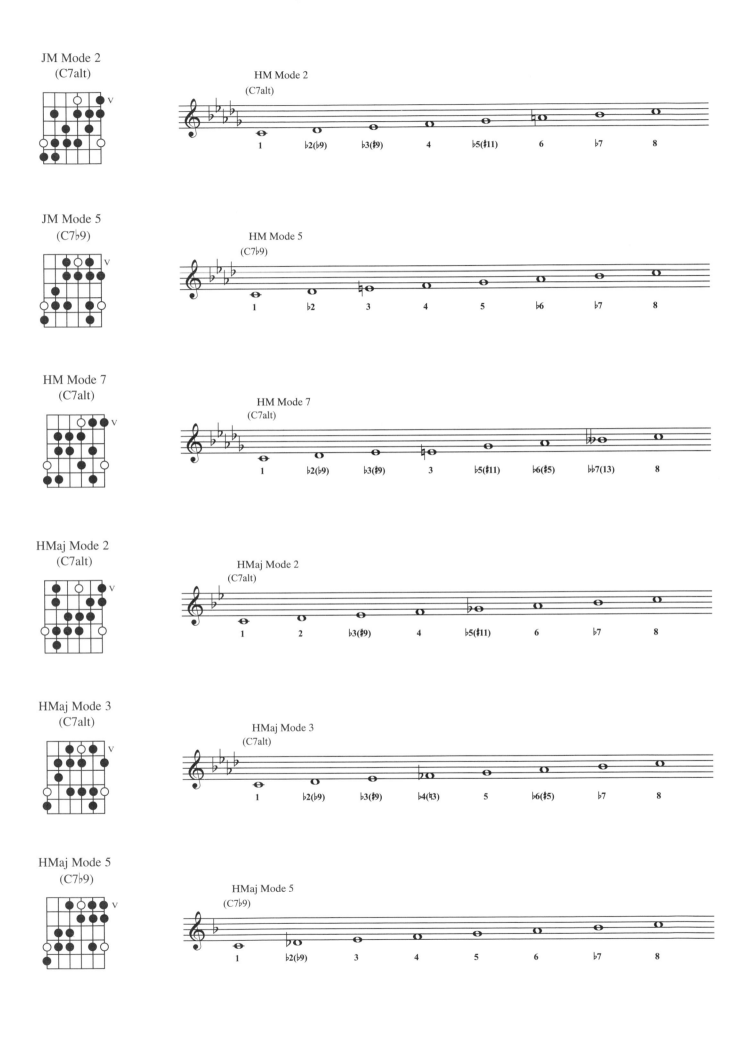

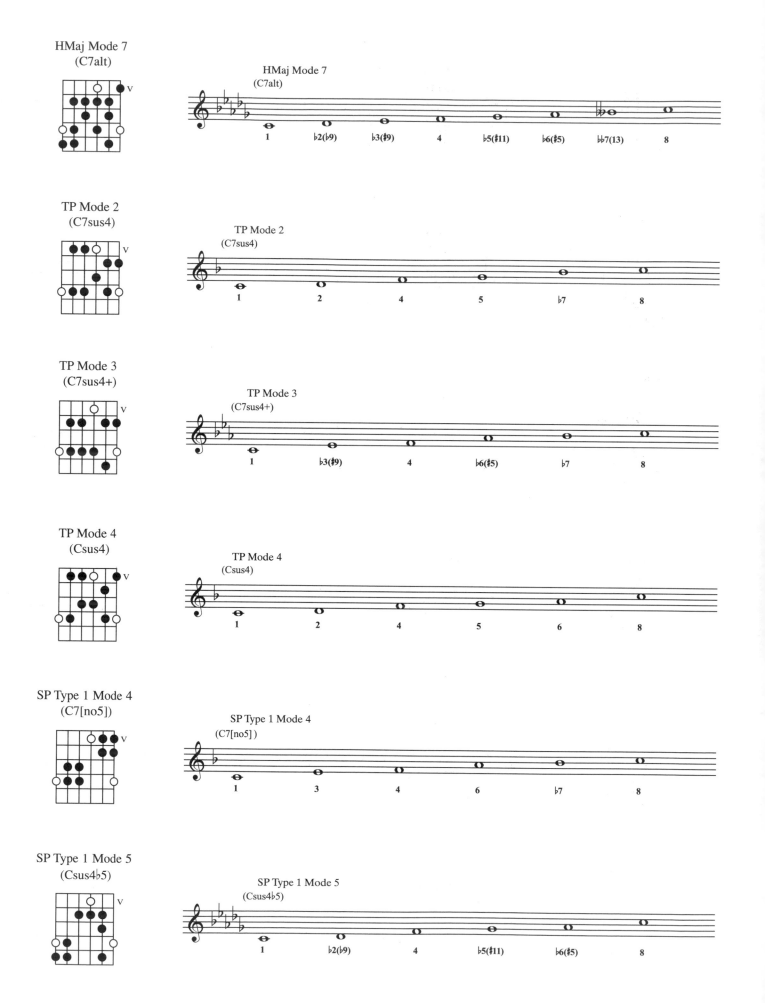

HMaj Mode 7
(C7alt)

HMaj Mode 7
(C7alt)

1   ♭2(♭9)   ♭3(♯9)   4   ♭5(♯11)   ♭6(♯5)   ♭♭7(13)   8

TP Mode 2
(C7sus4)

TP Mode 2
(C7sus4)

1   2   4   5   ♭7   8

TP Mode 3
(C7sus4+)

TP Mode 3
(C7sus4+)

1   ♭3(♯9)   4   ♭6(♯5)   ♭7   8

TP Mode 4
(Csus4)

TP Mode 4
(Csus4)

1   2   4   5   6   8

SP Type 1 Mode 4
(C7[no5])

SP Type 1 Mode 4
(C7[no5])

1   3   4   6   ♭7   8

SP Type 1 Mode 5
(Csus4♭5)

SP Type 1 Mode 5
(Csus4♭5)

1   ♭2(♭9)   4   ♭5(♯11)   ♭6(♯5)   8

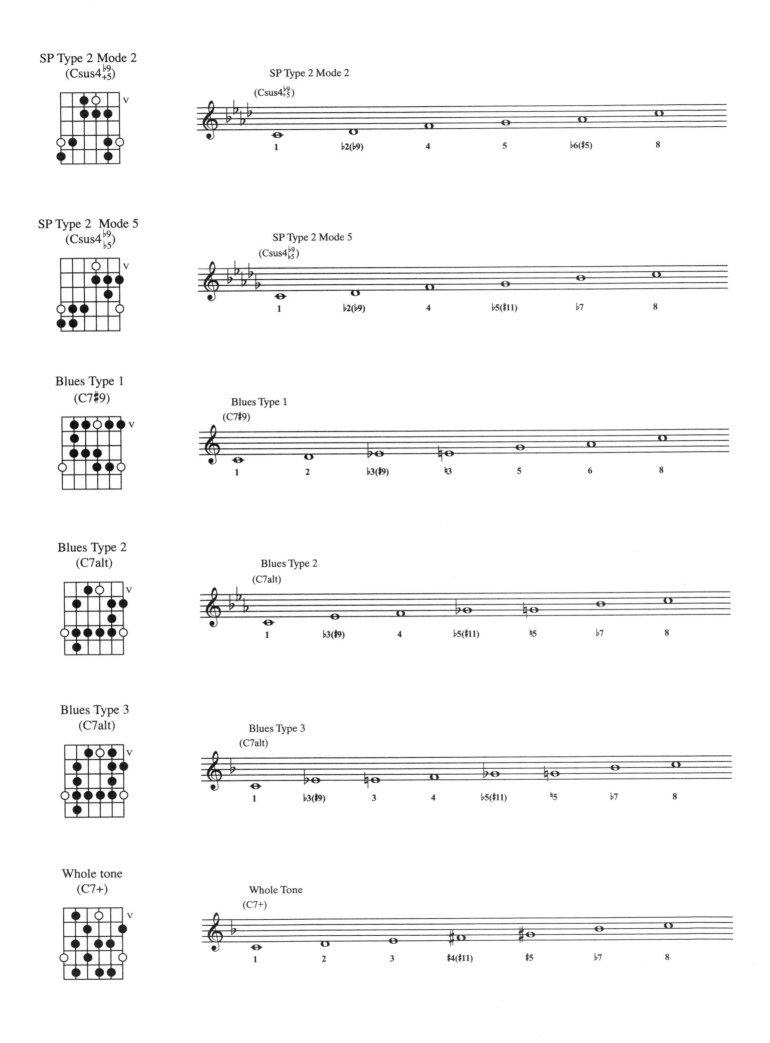

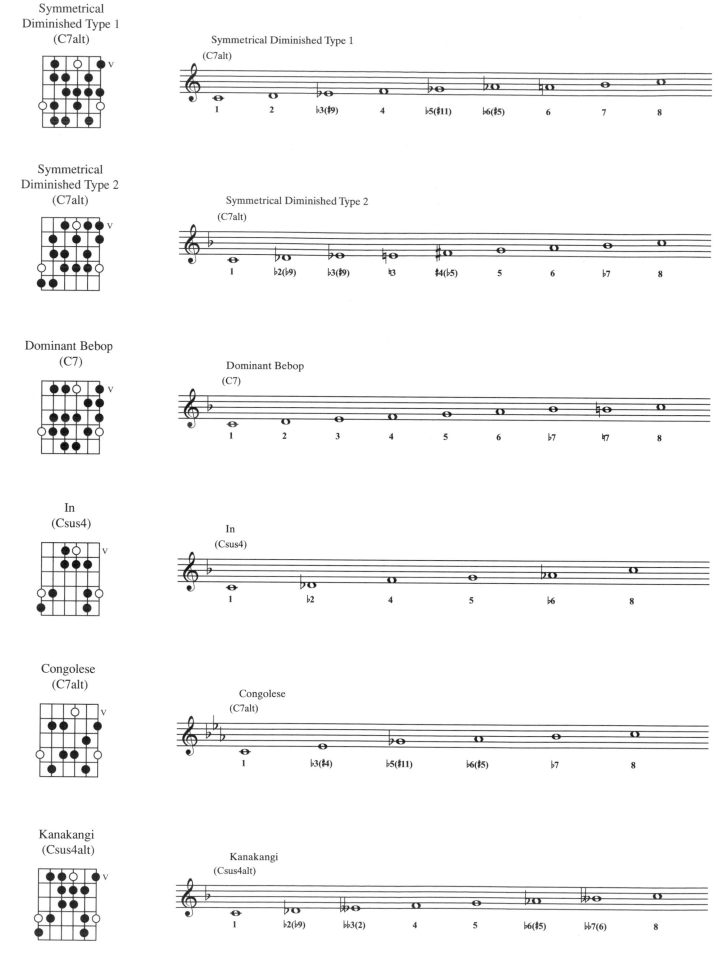

Conclusion

When you're at a party, you've got to know when to leave.
Miles Davis

Although this book has come to an end, the journey has no end. There are progressions that need be explored and themes yet to be composed. Again, your imagination is your only limitation. You don't need to memorize every scale, in every position, and in every key to master modes. Just take what you like and leave the rest. Learn a scale and begin applying it to your daily practice until it becomes part of your vocabulary.

We thank you for allowing us to share our experiences with you and hope that we have helped you understand the ambiguous subject of modal applications and, in the process, inspired you to further your musical development. Our hope is that you will refer to this book time and time again. (Especially when you feel that your playing is in a rut.) In addition, we encourage you to share what you've learned with others and keep the music alive.

We'll leave you with this closing thought:
Much to my own amazement, I still really love to play. It doesn't take much; I really enjoy just sitting in a room with my guitar and listening to or reading some music I can learn from.
Mike Stern

Good luck!

About the Authors

Ed Lozano is a professional guitarist and instructor. He has played professionally across the U.S. and Canada, written and produced music for film and television, and authored a three-book blues method for Amsco Publications. Ed also earned a B.F.A. in Commercial Arranging/Professional Writing from Boston's Berklee College of Music. Currently, he is producing a series of instructional CDs for the Latino community and researching Latin American folk music for future projects. Ed is also a member of ASCAP and the World Music Institute.

Ed Lozano uses and endorses Black Diamond Strings.

Joe Dineen has been playing guitar professionally for the last twenty years, and has been an instructor for the last fifteen. He has toured with countless bands playing rock, Motown, and oldies on both the East and West Coasts. He has written songs for many well-known performing artists, as well as source music for a number of feature films. He is currently writing music for an upcoming feature film, working on treatments for his next instructional book, and playing gigs in and around the New York Tri-State area.